Strategies for Struggling Readers

STEP BY STEP

Strategies for Struggling Readers

STEP BY STEP

Maria J. Meyerson
University of Nevada, Las Vegas

Dorothy L. Kulesza
Clark County School District

Merrill
Prentice Hall

Upper Saddle River, New Jersey
Columbus, Ohio

Library of Congress Cataloging-in-Publication Data

Meyerson, Maria J.
   Strategies for struggling readers : step by step / by Maria J. Meyerson and Dorothy Kulesza.
      p. cm.
   Includes bibliographical references.
   ISBN 0-13-022518-5
   1. Reading. I. Kulesza, Dorothy. II. Title.

 LB1573.M455 2002
 372.4—dc21

                                                                                    00-052528

Vice President and Publisher: Jeffery W. Johnston
Editor: Linda Ashe Montgomery
Production Editor: Mary M. Irvin
Design Coordinator: Diane C. Lorenzo
Project Coordination and Text Design: Carlisle Publisher Services
Cover Design: Linda Fares
Cover Photo: JAM Photo
Production Manager: Pamela D. Bennett
Director of Marketing: Kevin Flanagan
Marketing Manager: Krista Groshong
Marketing Coordinator: Barbara Kuontz

This book was set in Palatino by Carlisle Communications, Ltd., and was printed and bound by Courier Kendallville, Inc. The cover was printed by Phoenix Color Corp.

Prentice-Hall International (UK) Limited, *London*
Prentice-Hall of Australia Pty. Limited, *Sydney*
Prentice-Hall of Canada, Inc., *Toronto*
Prentice-Hall Hispanoamericana, S. A., *Mexico*
Prentice-Hall of India Private Limited, *New Delhi*
Prentice-Hall of Japan, Inc., *Tokyo*
Simon & Schuster Asia Pte. Ltd., *Singapore*
Editora Prentice-Hall do Brasil, Ltda., *Rio de Janeiro*

10 9 8 7 6 5 4 3 2 1
ISBN 0-13-022518-5

PREFACE

For many children in U.S. classrooms, learning to read does not happen automatically or easily. The reasons that children may struggle with reading are numerous. Regardless of the reasons, however, classroom teachers are faced with the responsibility of assisting each and every child to become literate.

Even the most successful readers may struggle with reading at times. Take, for example, the average adult trying to comprehend tax laws. Every year, millions of Americans file their income taxes. The complexity of the instructions and tax laws on which they are based put many literate adults at a disadvantage. Many of us solve this reading problem by hiring "experts" who specialize in this form of reading comprehension.

One way to consider the needs of struggling readers is in relationship to what the most successful readers do. Given any text that readers may encounter—from a grocery list to the most complex physics treatise—successful readers are motivated to complete the task; read with a fluency that results from automatic decoding; and comprehend the given text. When any one of these components is not at an optimal level, or a combination of them are out of sync, readers will struggle and likely be unsuccessful at their reading task.

To assist struggling readers we offer a number of research-based strategies. These strategies were used by a variety of teachers and tutors who work with children at the Literacy Development Center at the University of Nevada, Las Vegas or the Paradise Professional Development School. We have changed the names of the children described in the book, however, to protect their privacy.

To facilitate your use of the strategies we provide in this text, we have organized them into four areas of literacy: *motivation, word recognition, comprehension,* and *fluency.* These four areas of literacy, as well as the strategies described, work in unity. Improvement in one area will most likely improve another area. You will note that we have also grouped the strategies based on an understanding that their "power" will influence and promote success in other literacy areas. Finally, we have included references and additional information to assist teachers in expanding and modifying the strategies for their own teaching situations.

We wish to thank our families, friends, and Linda Scharp McElhiney, who encouraged us to write this book. Most important, we wish to thank the children and students we teach; they continue to help us refine our practices.

We also wish to thank the reviewers of our manuscript for their comments and insights: Alexander Casareno, The University of Portland; Karen Cole, The University of North Carolina–Asheville; David C. Little, Samford University; William J. Oehlkers, Rhode Island College; Tobie R. Sanders, Capital University; and Marla Slack, The University of Phoenix.

Maria J. Meyerson
Dorothy "Dottie" Kulesza

■ CONTENTS ■

■ PART IV

When Struggling Readers Need to Improve Fluency   69

■ PART V

Assessing Children Who May Be Struggling with Reading   83

■ APPENDIX

Additional Forms   97

NOTE: Every effort has been made to provide accurate and current Internet information in this book. However, the Internet and information posted on it are constantly changing, so it is inevitable that some of the Internet addresses listed in this textbook will change.

■ ABOUT THE AUTHORS ■

Maria J. Meyerson, Ph.D., is a professor of literacy education at the University of Nevada, Las Vegas (UNLV). She is a former remedial reading teacher. Over the past 16 years at UNLV she has worn many hats, including Director of the Literacy Development Center. Most recently, she has been very involved with the establishment of the Paradise Professional Development School, where she works with UNLV preservice teachers and mentor teachers.

Dorothy L. Kulesza, M.Ed., called "Dottie" by all who know her, is reading specialist at the Paradise Professional Development School as well as a former classroom teacher. She is also a part-time literacy instructor at UNLV. At the time of this printing, Dottie is well on her way to completing her doctoral degree.

PART I

When Struggling Readers Need to Improve Interest, Attitude, and Motivation

Before we begin implementing our strategies for improved word recognition, comprehension, and fluency, we believe that it is essential to first address struggling readers' affective needs as they relate to motivation as well as what teachers can do to enhance student motivation. Struggling readers often sit in classrooms where they have probably not had much opportunity to feel successful in literacy. They sit among proficient readers who rapidly recognize words, read aloud with smooth and fluent expression, and participate in book discussions. Struggling readers are frequently presented with teacher-selected materials, either grade-level selections that are too difficult for them or below-grade level materials in which they have no interest.

While teachers hope that children will be intrinsically motivated to engage in literacy, we need to demonstrate to struggling readers how to be self-motivated through the incorporation of choice, control, challenge, and purpose into the daily classroom routines (Ames, 1992; Gambrell, 1996; Oldfather, 1993; Pintrich & Schunk, 1996; Turner & Paris, 1995). Figure 1.1 shows the interrelationship between the components of motivation. Teachers who are mindful of these interrelationships will help struggling readers be successful through explicit instruction in how to choose reading materials for specific purposes and thus give students control and appropriate challenge over their own reading.

The classroom climate is an important element to consider for nurturing students' motivation to read and write. If you have ever watched youngsters as they play video games, you will notice that they seem to be in another world as they engage in the fast action of the latest video craze. In a real sense they are in another world; they have entered a state of total concentration and are one with the game. These optimal

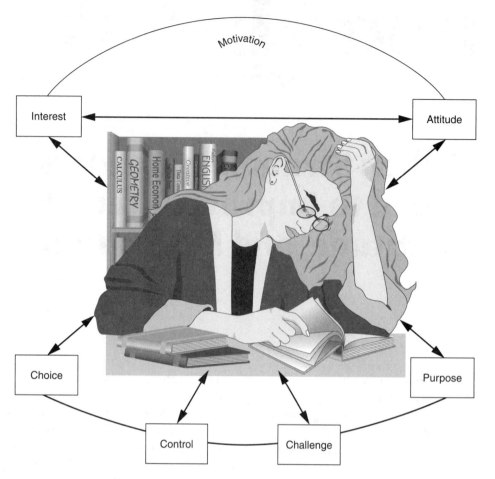

FIGURE 1.1   Components of Motivation.

experiences (Csikszentmihalyi, 1990) can happen to everyone when we are engaged in meaningful activities and enter a state of "flow."

> Flow tends to happen when a person faces a clear set of goals that require appropriate responses. It is easy to enter flow in games such as chess, tennis, or poker because they have goals and rules for action that make it possible for the player to act without questioning what should be done, and how (Csikszentmihalyi, 1997, p. 29).

Avid readers often experience flow; they literally get lost in a book (Nell, 1988). They become part of the story and lose track of the world around them. Writers, artists, and athletes also describe this pleasurable state of being. The activities may be challenging and difficult, but individuals continue to engage in them to experience the flow.

Classrooms that promote flow are child-centered. Teachers design classroom environments so that children are free to engage in activities of interest to them. For struggling readers, interaction with print that sustains their interests is paramount. So, too, is the time given to pursue interests. In order for flow to occur in the classroom, children must be given the time it takes to enter this state.

Teachers can create a classroom climate that promotes flow by:

1. Establishing a classroom environment that is child-centered. Provide children the opportunity to make choices whenever possible—choice in what to read and write and choice in method of response.

2. Providing classroom time to engage in activities that require students to concentrate and focus. Sustained silent reading and readers/writers workshop are two teaching practices that will help children get in the flow if they are used regularly. Research projects that require children to read reference materials, use the Internet, or study maps also are excellent opportunities for flow. Allow classroom time for projects instead of assigning them for homework.

3. Minimizing interruptions. Keep track of the number of times children interrupt each other as well as how often you interrupt them. If interruptions are excessive, modify your procedures.

■ THE GOLDILOCKS PLAN

Choice in literacy activities is a component of reading motivation (Oldfather, 1993; Gambrell, 1996; Sweet & Guthrie, 1996; Guthrie & Wigfield, 1997). Several decades ago, Veatch (1959) suggested that students should self-select reading materials and stressed the importance of teaching selection strategies. The Goldilocks strategy for selecting books was outlined by Ohlhausen and Jepsen (1992). Students are taught, in a series of mini-lessons and individual conferences, how to classify their book selections as too hard, too easy, or just right. A book that was too hard was described as one that the student really wanted to read but knew was too difficult at the time. A book that was just right was one that the student wanted to read and could read, while finding only one or two unknown words per page. A book that was too easy was an old favorite, read many times before.

The Power of the Strategy for Struggling Readers

Struggling readers select books that are too difficult for a variety of reasons: (a) the books are about a topic in which they are interested; (b) the books are widely read by their peers, and they want to be part of the reading club; and (c) selection strategies have not been discussed with them. The latter is also one of the reasons that they select books that are too easy, along with the fact that these books provide a comfortable and successful experience. Providing struggling readers with the Goldilocks strategy allows them to:

1. Feel confident in their ability to read their self-selected books
2. Improve their skills through increased reading experiences
3. Read a wider variety of texts

Steps to Follow

1. Introduce the concept of too hard, too easy, and just right books.
2. Model using your own books, showing examples of books that are too hard, too easy, and just right for you to read.
3. Have the students spend time exploring each of these categories of books for themselves.
4. In the classroom library, post the questions the students should ask themselves when selecting books using the Goldilocks Plan.

A book is too hard if you answer "yes" to these questions:

1. Are there more than two words on a page you don't know?
2. Are you confused about what is happening in most of this book?
3. When you read, does it sound pretty choppy?
4. Is everyone else too busy and unable to help you?

A book is too easy if you answer "yes" to these questions:

1. Have you read it many, many times before?
2. Do you understand the story very, very well?
3. Do you know (understand, pronounce) almost every word?
4. Can you read it smoothly?

A book is just right if you answer "yes" to these questions:

1. Is this book new to you?
2. Do you understand some of this book?
3. Are there just one or two words per page that you don't know?

Application and Examples

Introduce the Goldilocks strategy with a read-aloud of a familiar version of *Goldilocks and the Three Bears*. Continue to reinforce the use of the Goldilocks Plan during small group or individual conferences. Encourage students to discuss their recent selections, and the strategies they used for choosing them, with you and with their peers. Make an audiotape of an alternative Goldilocks story, for example, *The Dumb Bunnies, Goldilocks and the Three Hares,* or *Somebody and the Three Blairs*. At the end of the tape, once again remind the students of the Goldilocks Plan; have them write about one of their recent selections and how it fit the criteria. Put the tape at a listening center with multiple copies of the book.

Teaching Aids

Once teachers have introduced the Goldilocks Plan to students, periodic checks with those children who tend to have difficulty choosing their books may still be necessary. A chart such as the one presented in Figure 1.2 can be made and posted in the classroom to help remind children of how to select books.

The Goldilocks Plan

Is your book too hard, too easy or just right for you?

Use the Goldilocks Plan to find out! Ask yourself these questions.

FIGURE 1.2 The Goldilocks Plan. (Ohlhausen, M. M., & Jepsen, M. (1992). Lessons from Goldilocks: "Somebody's been choosing my books but I can make my own choices now!" *The New Advocate 5*, 31–46.

Continued

Too Hard?

If you answer "yes," this book is probably "too hard" for you. Give this book another try in a few months.

1. Are there more than two words on a page that you don't know?

2. Are you confused about what is happening in the book?

3. When you try to read a part out loud, does it sound choppy?

4. Will you have to ask someone to help with the book many times?

FIGURE 1.2 Continued

Just Right?

If you answer "yes," this book is probably "just right" for you.
Go ahead. Read and learn from it.

1. Is this a new book for you?

2. Do you understand some of the book?

3. Are there just one or two words on a page that you don't know?

4. When you read out loud are some parts smooth and some choppy?

5. If you need help, will it just be now and then? Who can help you?

FIGURE 1.2 Continued

Too Easy?

If you answer "yes," this book is probably "too easy" for you. Have fun with it!

1. Have you read this book many, many times before?

2. Do you understand the story very well and can you tell someone about it almost as if you were the author?

3. Do you know how to say almost every word and what every word means?

4. Can you read the book out loud very smoothly?

FIGURE 1.2 Concluded

■ TALK, TALK, TALK

Engaged readers are those who are motivated, knowledgeable, strategic, and socially interactive (Baumann & Duffy, 1997). Sharing and communicating with others while constructing and extending the meaning of text provides the social interaction component of reading engagement (Gambrell, 1996). Students should talk, talk, talk about their reading experiences. The Conversational Discussion Group (O'Flahavan, 1989; O'Flahavan & Stein, 1992; O'Flahavan, Stein, Wiencek, & Marks, 1992) provides a structure for students to discuss literature. The teacher's role, once the framework is established, is to present questions that prompt the discussion and then leave the group and let the conversation begin. The teacher is then available as a resource when the students need one.

The Power of the Strategy for Struggling Readers

One component of the framework for the Conversational Discussion Group is a set of rules for interaction. These rules create a format that allows each student to have equal participation in the discussion. The struggling reader, whose voice is often lost in a large group discussion controlled by the teacher, has an opportunity to talk with peers. In a small group discussion with a set of rules and a focus for text interpretation, the struggling readers can see themselves on an equal playing field with their peers.

Steps to Follow

1. Make a chart, using student input, listing guidelines for interaction. Some examples are: Everyone gets a chance to talk; Do not interrupt the speaker; Pay attention to the speaker; and Stay on the subject (Figure 1.3).
2. Brainstorm with the students different ways to interpret text and list these in another column on the chart. They can interpret the text by

FIGURE 1.3   Chart for Literature Discussion.

Guidelines for Interactions	Ways to Interpret Text
Everyone gets a chance to talk	Think about the:
Do not interrupt the speaker	Characters
Pay attention to the speaker	Setting
Stay on the subject	Illusions
	Point of view

examining the characters, setting, and illustrations, and the point of view taken by the author.

3. To begin a group's discussion, introduce/review the format as outlined on the chart.

4. Pose three questions, based on the text, to the group. The first question should be designed to activate prior knowledge or personal experiences that connect to the selection. The second question should lead the students into the text; and the third should lead to an extension of it.

5. Leave the group and let the discussion begin. Let the students know that you will be available if they have a question. Remain nearby, taking notes on interpretation strategies that are used (see Figure 1.4).

6. When the peer discussion is over, return to the group for a debriefing. Revisit the chart during the debriefing to check for guidelines that were followed and interpretation strategies that were used. Discuss what could be done to improve the next discussion.

Application and Examples

After creating the chart with the guidelines for interaction and interpretation, introduce the Conversational Discussion Group procedure with a read-aloud. Read Patricia Polacco's *Thundercake*. Review the guidelines and then pose the three questions. For example: "How do you feel when there's a thunderstorm in the distance, and it's coming your way?"; "How did the grandmother's attitude about the storm affect the little girl?"; and "What did we learn from this story?"

Teaching Aids

A chart such as the one presented in Figure 1.4 may be used for record-keeping of the interpretation strategies used by the students. This will assist the teacher in helping struggling readers expand their interpretation repertoire.

◼ BOOK STACKING

Blachowicz and Wimett (1994) reported using this strategy with preservice teachers who in turn used it with elementary and middle school students. A wide array of books is collected by the teacher (at least three per student), and the books are placed in varied stacks on each student chair in the classroom. The students are given time to browse the stacks and then sit by a stack that contains at least one book that they would like to read. This strategy provides choice and fosters social interaction for the students; it also provides information on student interests for the teacher.

Discussion Group—Interpretation Strategies

Student	Date	Title of Selection	Character	Setting	Point of View	Illustrations	

FIGURE 1.4 Interpretation Strategies Chart.

The Power of the Strategy for Struggling Readers

Book stacking provides a structure that nourishes the motivation to read. Used as an introductory activity, the struggling readers can select books with which they have some familiarity. This will provide them with an opportunity to:

1. Demonstrate their reading interests
2. Feel confident in their ability to read the selection
3. Have a successful reading experience from the on-set
4. Participate in a book discussion

Steps to Follow

1. The teacher selects a large assortment of books that depict a wide variety of interests, genres, and reading levels. There should be a minimum of three books per student.
2. A varied stack of books is placed on each student chair in the classroom.
3. The students are given a browsing time of 15 to 20 minutes.
4. When students find a book that they would like to read, they sit by that stack.
5. A discussion of selections is held with students explaining why they chose a particular book/stack.
6. The teacher can note the selections of each student to facilitate gathering reading materials of interest to the students in the future.

Application and Examples

Following the initial Book Stacking activity, students could pair up or form small groups with others who have similar interests. They could buddy read, trade books, hold book discussions, or investigate new books of interest together. A variation of the activity in which the students make the stacks was reported by Blachowicz and Wimett (1994). The students created stacks of books that they believed would be selected by characters in books and then explained their choices in discussion groups.

Teaching Aids

For the elementary classroom, select books from a wide range of reading levels. Be sure to include books from all genres and try to address a variety of interests. See Figure 1.5 for suggestions.

FIGURE 1.5 Suggested
Groupings for Bookstacking.

Beginner Books	Familiar titles	Popular Series
Wordless picture books	Fairy Tales	Bailey School Kids
Dr. Seuss titles	Mother Goose	The Littles
Predictable stories	Frog and Toad	Babysitters Club
Rhyming stories	Amelia Bedelia	Boxcar Children
Leveled books	Horrible Harry	Goosebumps
Popular favorites	**Informational**	**Just-for-fun**
Eric Carle	Animals	Jokes
Shel Silverstein	Space	Riddles
Jack Prelutsky	Sports	Scary stories
Roald Dahl	Famous people	Tall tales
Shiloh	How-to books	Legends
Charlotte's Web	Magic School Bus	Fables/Myths

■ LITERACY AND COMPUTERS

Some computer programs can serve as a motivational springboard for a struggling reader or writer. A fifth grader who was being tutored at the University of Nevada, Las Vegas (UNLV) Literacy Development Center looked forward with anticipation to writing summaries of his reading, using the My Own Stories software. This program allows the user to design illustrations by selecting from a wide range of possible sites, people, animals, objects, and furniture. The student, who was reading *My Side of the Mountain* with his tutor, would painstakingly recreate a scene as described by the author. Knowing that he would have the opportunity to use this program motivated him to read carefully for details of the setting and actions of the plot. After creating the scene to his satisfaction, he would then write a brief summary of the story to accompany it. Even without access to a particular software program, the classroom computer can be used to this advantage with the struggling reader. Try using the basic clip art or drawing portions of the word processing program that is installed on your classroom computer.

The Power of the Strategy for Struggling Readers

Struggling readers are often as limited in their use of classroom computers as they are in other literacy activities. Their peers are able to use the classroom computer for research, communication, reading, and writing. The struggling reader is often unable to conduct research on the computer because the accessed information is written at grade level or above. The struggling reader, who is often a struggling writer, requires constant monitoring or assistance in composing an electronic communication, as well as reading back any received response. Providing a format for the student to work independently on the computer, while at the same time connecting reading and writing, may provide just the right motivational spark.

Steps to Follow

1. Preview the available clip art and provide instruction for use of the drawing program on your classroom computer.
2. Provide time for the struggling readers to become familiar with both of these computer components.
3. Read a book with your students and then model the creation of illustrations of the setting and characters using the clip art or drawing program. Complete the process by composing with them a few sentences that accompany the illustrations, while summarizing the storyline of the book.
4. Monitor the struggling readers as they complete the same process with a book read either independently or in a guided reading lesson.
5. Add this computer component to the repertoire of motivational strategies available for use by your struggling readers.

Application and Examples

Read *The Night I Followed the Dog* with your struggling readers. Discuss the different settings, characters, and actions. Gather around the computer and together brainstorm the available clip art, selecting ones that could appropriately be used with this book. Using this lesson for modeling the procedure, Dottie and her intermediate reading students created a summary page with clip art from the Student Writing Center (Figure 1.6).

Teaching Aids

Many of the books designed for struggling readers, especially those leveled by Reading Recovery levels, are conducive to use for this activity with basic clip art. The characters are often family members or common animals, and the situations are often familiar ones such as birthday parties. As the struggling readers progress through books that provide less picture support, they should be encouraged to return to the text for words and phrases that describe the characters and settings.

In addition to Student Writing Center, other programs that are often installed on classroom computers that work very well for this strategy are ClarisWorks for Kids and Kid Pix. The following references may be useful for the classroom teacher:

ClarisWorks for Kids [Computer software]. (1997). Gresham, OR: Vision Technology in Education.

We read *The Night I Followed the Dog* by Nina Laden.

The boy used to think that his dog was boring. Then one night he followed him from the dog house into the city. The boy found out that his dog had a very exciting life at night.

FIGURE 1.6   Using Clip Art to Summarize a Story.

George, J. C. (1959). *My side of the mountain.* New York: Scholastic.

Kid Pix [Computer software]. (1994). Novato, CA: Broderbund.

Laden, Nina. (1994). *The night I followed the dog.* New York: Scholastic.

My Own Stories [Computer software]. (1993). MECC.

Student Writing Center [Computer software]. (1993). Fremont, CA: The Learning Company.

■ OTHER MEDIA

There may be other equipment available in the classroom that can motivate struggling readers. Sometimes useful equipment can be borrowed from elsewhere in the school building or brought in from home. For equipment that could be shared throughout a grade level or school, perhaps it could be purchased through fund raising, grant writing, or the school budget itself. The overhead projector, common equipment in almost every classroom, can be used by students instead of being a tool only for use by the teacher. Photography from the teacher's personal camera brought from home or from one purchased for the classroom can be used in a variety of ways by students. The music and art specialists can be called upon to offer their expertise and loan some equipment or supplies for motivational activities. A piece of equipment that could be shared throughout the school would be a karaoke machine that can be integrated with the classroom television set.

The Power of the Strategy for Struggling Readers

Unable to complete grade-level work, struggling readers are often given worksheets to take up their time. They work on fill-in-the blank skill sheets; they match and color beginning sounds, prefixes, synonyms, antonyms, and homonyms. Using some of the other media allows the struggling readers to use their creative senses, which may, at the moment, be more highly developed than their literacy skills.

Steps to Follow

1. Give the students markers and transparencies and have them work together or individually to make a web of their prior knowledge and/or their predictions for a book that they are about to read. Let them use transparencies for book responses, drawing or writing the characters, setting, or plot actions; provide time for the students to share with the class. One of Dottie's third-grade reading students concisely summarized in one sentence a book that he had read and made it a caption for a transparency (Figure 1.7) to share with his class.

2. Use a classroom camera to provide actual photographs taken of or by the students to inspire reading and writing. Take the students for an environment walk around the school grounds, taking pictures for them to use for research, reading, or writing activities. Take pictures of school personnel and then let your students interview them to write captions or biographies to go along with the photographs. Brainstorm with the students what questions they could ask during their interviews. For a biography, a sample interview questionnaire is included in Figure 1. 8.

3. Gather children's books that use different media for illustrations. Ask the art specialist for assistance with materials and methods. Set up centers in your classroom supplied with different art materials with which your students can experiment. Keep the materials on hand for when students are ready to illustrate their own books. Examples of illustrative techniques that could be used for art centers are: watercolors, cut paper, collage, pastels, scratchboard, colored pencils, and woodcuts.

4. Borrow several different hand-held instruments from the music department. Try using them with books that have repetitive phrases. Assign an instrument to each character or action that is repeated throughout the story. Each time the word for the character or action is read, the student makes the musical sound with the instrument.

5. Find access to a karaoke machine that can be interfaced with your classroom television set. Let the music begin, with the lyrics running across the TV screen; see how motivated those struggling readers will be to read the words to the song along with their peers.

FIGURE 1.7   An Example of a Student-made Transparency.

Application and Example

A number of different art centers for book illustrations can be developed through the school year for students to explore as they are further motivated to read.

Watercolors

For the watercolor center, gather tempera paints from your art teacher, or purchase inexpensive watercolor paints at your local department store. Add brushes, cups of water, and paper. For examples of watercolor illustrations, gather some of the following picture books:

Mirette on the Highwire, written and illustrated by Emily Arnold McCully

The Patchwork Quilt, written by Valerie Flournoy, illustrated by Jerry Pinkney

Strega Nona, written and illustrated by Tomie de Paola

Grandfather's Journey, written and illustrated by Allen Say

Tuesday, written and illustrated by David Wiesner

Cousin Ruth's Tooth, written by Amy MacDonald, illustrated by Marjorie Priceman

Interviewer: _____   Interviewee: _____

1. What is your job at our school?

2. Where were you born?

3. Where did you go to elementary school?

4. What was your favorite grade?

5. Who was your favorite teacher?

6. What did you like most about school?

7. Why did you want to work in a school?

8. What's the best part about being in our school?

9. What are your hobbies?

10. Do you have any children?

11. What does your family do for fun?

12. Is there anything about yourself that you would like to add?

FIGURE 1.8   Biography Interview Questionnaire.

Peppe the Lamplighter, written by Elisa Bartone, illustrated by Ted Lewin

When I Was Young in the Mountains, written by Cynthia Rylant, illustrated by Diane Goode

Cecil's Story, written by George Ella Lyon, illustrated by Peter Catalanotto

Possum Magic, written by Mem Fox, illustrated by Julie Vivas

The Talking Eggs: A Folktale from the American South, retold by Robert D. San Souci, illustrated by Jerry Pinkney

Cut Paper

For the cut paper center, gather a variety of types of paper available in your school. There can be construction paper, writing paper, tissue paper, and white and colored photocopy paper. Add scissors and glue or rubber cement to complete the center. For examples of cut paper illustrations, gather some of the following picture books:

The Golem, written and illustrated by David Wisniewski

Rain Player, written and illustrated by David Wisniewski

Elfwyn's Saga: Story and Pictures, written by David Wisniewski, illustrated by Lee Salsbery

The Warrior and the Wise Man, written and illustrated by David Wisniewski

Harlem, written by Walter Dean Myers, illustrated by Christopher Myers

Saint Valentine, written and illustrated by Robert Sabuda

Once Upon Another, written and illustrated by Suse MacDonald and Bill Oakes

Numblers, written and illustrated by Suse MacDonald and Bill Oakes

Mouse Paint, written and illustrated by Ellen Stoll Walsh

The Emperor and the Kite, written by Jane Yolen, illustrated by Ed Young

Color Zoo, written and illustrated by Lois Ehlert

Chicka Chicka Boom Boom, written by John Archambault and Bill Martin, Jr., illustrated by Lois Ehlert

Fish Eyes A Book You Can Count On, written and illustrated by Lois Ehlert

Collage

For the collage center, gather a variety of materials. Surprisingly, you may find many of them right in your classroom. Think about materials you've gathered for other projects across the curriculum. There was probably a little bit of this and a little bit of that left over that you didn't want to throw away. Some extra materials can be found taking a walk around the school grounds. The collage center can include just about anything: paper, fabric, yarn, ribbon, seeds, twigs, pebbles, cottonballs, craft sticks, plastic wrap, bottle caps, broken pencils, etc. Add glue and scissors to complete the center. For examples of collage illustrations, gather some of the following picture books:

The Very Hungry Caterpillar, written and illustrated by Eric Carle

The Very Quiet Cricket, written and illustrated by Eric Carle

Smoky Night, written by Eve Bunting, illustrated by David Diaz

Peter's Chair, written and illustrated by Ezra Jack Keats

Goggles, written and illustrated by Ezra Jack Keats

The Snowy Day, written and illustrated by Ezra Jack Keats

Where the Forest Meets the Sea, written and illustrated by Jeannie Baker

Inch by Inch, written and illustrated by Leo Lionni

Arrow to the Sun: A Pueblo Indian Tale, adapted and illustrated by Gerald McDermott

Pastels

The pastels might be available from your art specialist or from your school supplies. If not, they can be purchased at your local arts and craft store. Otherwise, you can use colored chalk, readily available and much less expensive. Add paper for the background and a box of tissues to complete the center. For examples of pastel illustrations, gather some of the following picture books:

Lon Po Po: A Red-Riding Hood Story from China, translated and illustrated by Ed Young

Hoops, written by Robert Burleigh, illustrated by Stephen T. Johnson

While I Sleep, written by Mary Calhoun, illustrated by Ed Young

Whoo-oo Is It?, written by Megan McDonald, illustrated by S. D. Schindler

The Sleepytime Book, written by Jan Wahl, illustrated by Arden Johnson

The Samurai's Daughter: A Japanese Legend, retold by Robert D. San Souci, illustrated by Stephen T. Johnson

Chin Yu Min and the Ginger Cat, written by Jennifer Armstrong, illustrated by Mary Grandpre

Haircuts at Sleepy Sam's, written by Michael R. Strickland, illustrated by Keaf Holliday

Angels in the Dust, written by Margot Theis Raven, illustrated by Roger Essley

Scratchboard

The scratchboard art center can be simply equipped with all colors of crayons and extra black. To acquire the effect of the scratchboard technique, the students color a paper and then color over it with black crayon. Almost anything available in the classroom (scissors, a blunt pencil, an opened paper clip, the edge of a ruler, etc.) could then be used to scratch off the black to create a picture. Kits for this activity can be purchased at your local teacher/educator supply store. For examples of scratchboard illustrations, gather some of the following picture books:

The Elephant's Wrestling Match, written by Judy Sierra, illustrated by Brian Pinkney

The Ballad of Belle Dorcas, written by William Hooks, illustrated by Brian Pinkney

Where Does the Trail Lead?, written by Albert Burton, illustrated by Brian Pinkney

The Faithful Friend, written by Robert D. San Souci, illustrated by Brian Pinkney

Sukey and the Mermaid, written by Robert D. San Souci, illustrated by Brian Pinkney

The Gettysburg Address, illustrated by Michael McCurdy

Giants in the Land, written by Diana Appelbaum, illustrated by Michael McCurdy

The Beasts of Bethlehem, verse by X. J. Kennedy, illustrated by Michael McCurdy

Duke Ellington, written by Andrea Davis Pinkney, illustrated by Brian Pinkney

Colored Pencils

A variety of colored pencils and white paper is all that is needed for this art center. For examples of colored pencil illustrations, gather some of the following picture books:

Frogs, Toads, Lizards, and Salamanders, written and illustrated by Nancy Winslow Parker and Joan R. Wright

Puss in Boots, written by Charles Perrault, translated by Malcolm Arthur, and illustrated by Fred Marcellino

Fenwick's Suit, written and illustrated by David Small

Song and Dance Man, written by Karen Ackerman, illustrated by Stephen Gammell

Waiting for the Whales, written by Sheryl McFarlane, illustrated by Ron Lightburn

The Cat & The Fiddle & More, written by Jim Aylesworth, illustrated by Richard Hull

Wolf Plays Alone, written and illustrated by Dominic Catalano

We're Making Breakfast for Mother, written by Shirley Neitzel, illustrated by Nancy Winslow Parker

It's Disgusting-And We Ate It!: True Food Facts From Around the World, written by James Solheim, illustrated by Eric Brace

Woodcuts

For the woodcut art center, let the students experiment with the medium, using Styrofoam materials (Laughlin & Watt, 1986). Save those Styrofoam packaging trays from the grocery store, or purchase some plates of that material. Borrow a brayer from your art teacher, or purchase an inexpensive mini-paint roller from your department store. Add India ink or paint, pencils, and construction paper to complete the center. The students draw a picture on the Styrofoam with a pencil, making sure that their marks are deeply indented. Next, they use the roller to cover the picture with paint or India ink. The last step is to put a piece of construction paper over the picture; this will provide a print which is the opposite of the picture drawn on the plate. For examples of woodcut illustrations, gather some of the following picture books:

> *Drummer Hoff,* adapted by Barbara Emberley, illustrated by Ed Emberley
>
> *A Story A Story: An African Tale,* written and illustrated by Gail E. Haley
>
> *Ever Heard of an Aardwolf?,* written by Madeline Moser, illustrated by Barry Moser
>
> *Swan Sky,* written and illustrated by Keizaburo Tejima
>
> *The Devils Who Learned to Be Good,* written and illustrated by Michael McCurdy
>
> *Antler, Bear, Canoe:* A Northwoods Alphabet Year, written and illustrated by Betsy Bowen
>
> *The Dancing Palm Tree And Other Nigerian Folktales,* written by Barbara K. Walker, illustrated by Helen Siegl
>
> *Bayberry Bluff,* written and illustrated by Blair Lent

PROFESSIONAL REFERENCES FOR IMPROVING INTEREST, ATTITUDE, AND MOTIVATION

Ames, C. (1992). Classrooms: Goals, structures, and student motivation. *Journal of Educational Psychology, 84*(3), 261–271.

Baumann, J. F., & Duffy, A. M. (1997). *Engaged reading for pleasure and learning: A report from the National Reading Research Center.* Athens, GA: NRRC.

Blachowicz, C. L. Z., & Wimett, C. A. (1994). Response to literature: Models for new teachers. In E. H. Cramer & M. Castle (Eds.), *Fostering the love of reading* (pp. 183–195). Newark, DE: IRA.

Csikszentmihalyi, M. (1990). *Flow: The psychology of optimal experiences.* New York: Harper & Row.

Csikszentmihalyi, M. (1997). *Finding flow; The psychology of engagement with everyday life.* New York: Basic Books.

Gambrell, L. B. (1996). Creating classroom cultures that foster reading motivation. *The Reading Teacher, 50*(1), 14–25.

Guthrie, J. T., & Wigfield, A. (Eds.). (1997). *Reading engagement: Motivating readers through integrated instruction.* Newark, DE: IRA.

Laughlin, M. K., & Watt, L. S. (1986). *Developing learning skills through children's literature: An idea book for K–5 classrooms and libraries.* Phoenix: Oryx Press.

Nell, V. (1988). *Lost in a book: The psychology of reading for pleasure.* New Haven, CT: Yale University Press.

O'Flahavan, J. F. (1989). *Second graders' social, intellectual, and affective development in varied group discussions about literature: An exploration of participation structure.* Unpublished doctoral dissertation, University of Illinois, Urbana-Champaign.

O'Flahavan, J. F., & Stein, C. (1992). In search of the teacher's role in peer discussions about literature. *Reading in Virginia, 12,* 34–42.

O'Flahavan, J. F., Stein, C., Wiencek, J., & Marks, T. (1992). *Intellectual development in peer discussions about literature: An exploration of the teacher's role (Final Report).* Urbana, IL: National Council of Teachers of English.

Ohlhausen, M. M., & Jepsen, M. (1992). Lessons from Goldilocks: "Somebody's been choosing my books but I can make my own choices now!" *The New Advocate, 5,* 31–46.

Oldfather, P. (1993). What students say about motivating experiences in a whole language classroom. *The Reading Teacher, 46*(8), 672–681.

Pintrich, P. R., & Schunk, D. H. (1996). *Motivation in education: Theory, research, and applications.* Englewood Cliffs, NJ: Prentice Hall.

Sweet, A. P., & Guthrie, J. T. (1996). How children's motivations relate to literacy development and instruction. *The Reading Teacher, 49*(8), 660–662.

Turner, J., & Paris, S. G. (1995). How literacy tasks influence children's motivation for literacy. *The Reading Teacher, 48*(8), 662–673.

Veatch, J. (1959). *Individualizing your reading program.* New York: G. P. Putnam's Sons.

PART II

When Struggling Readers Need to Improve Word Recognition

Word recognition, the ability to identify words through decoding, sight, context, configuration, or by other means, is one of the main components of literacy and is one of the areas that causes difficulty for struggling readers. Classroom teachers are well aware that all children at some time have difficulty recognizing some words. Struggling readers, however, often have a very limited sight vocabulary (words instantly recognized), over-rely on one recognition strategy (e.g., phonics) and/or fail to understand that meaning is inherent in the reading process, and therefore, word-call inaccurately (e.g., "house" for "horse").

Gipe (1995) suggests that that there are three types of word recognition difficulties related to instructional practices: (1) too much instruction in word recognition; (2) too little instruction in word recognition, and (3) unbalanced instruction in word recognition in that one strategy is emphasized over another. When we consider the big picture of literacy instruction, the notion of balance rings through all reasons for good instructional practices. The strategies presented here are included because they easily provide balanced instructional practice for children and incorporate reading, writing, listening, and speaking.

■ LANGUAGE EXPERIENCE APPROACH

While most references to the Language Experience Approach (LEA) (Allen, 1976; Hall, 1978) include in its definition the use with young children, it can be used successfully with older children who are struggling with learning to read as well as second language learners (Barr & Johnson, 1997). Its strengths as a teaching strategy are many:

1. Connection between the spoken and written word is made evident
2. The text created is based on students' own language
3. Teachers model sentence structure and the conventions of our language

Struggling readers, regardless of age, have many life experiences that teachers can tap to create text. It is important to recognize that some second language learners or children of poverty may have experiences that differ from the teachers' experiences or that they may offer a different perspective on the same experience. For example, a fifth-grade teacher who took a group of inner city students to another part of town to visit an art museum was amazed that most of the after-the-field-trip talk centered on the bus ride across town and the sights seen from the bus window rather than the art in the museum. The students had seen many paintings when the museum sent a traveling show to their school the previous year. The bus ride was the new experience that the teacher could capitalize on for a language experience story.

If a broad definition of LEA is employed, then the multitude of classroom experience provided through a student-centered, "hands-on" curriculum is fertile ground for language experience "stories," as well as the clarification of new concepts. Science and mathematics, in particular, provide students with new vocabulary and concepts that can be integrated into the LEA.

LEA can be used with individual students as well as with small groups. From a social constructivist perspective (Newman & Holzman, 1993), LEA can be very successful when students work together with a "more knowledgeable other." This person may be the teacher, a more experienced student, teacher aide, or parent.

The Power of the Strategy for Struggling Readers

The Language Experience Approach as it relates to word recognition provides teachers with an instructional framework to provide struggling readers with:

1. A way to reinforce the one-to-one correspondence between spoken and written language
2. A meaningful context based on children's knowledge and experience
3. Repeated readings of the same text as well as repetition of high-frequency words because these words are commonly used in our everyday speech
4. A meaning context to examine components of language (words, phonemes and morphemes)
5. Modeling of sentence structure by the teacher

Steps to Follow

1. Focus on an experience that is either common to all students in the group from outside their school experiences (e.g., going to the grocery store) or an experience that is the result of a class trip, class lesson, or activity.

2. Generate vocabulary that authors most likely would use if they were writing about the topic or idea.

3. Record students' dictation. Especially with young children, try not to rephrase students' sentences unless grammatical errors make text meaning confusing. With older students and adults, editing makes more sense.

4. Read text aloud, modeling fluency and making connections between speech and print by pointing to each word.

5. Invite students to read and reread the text orally and silently. This promotes fluency.

6. Once the complete text is known by the student or group, begin to focus on the smaller components of the text such as sentences, words, and letters. This will foster word recognition skills. Use sentence strips and word cards so students can manipulate text.

Application and Examples

The LEA can be used with an activity as easy to do as playing "Here We Go Round the Mulberry Bush" right in the classroom. Dottie recently played this game and then read a book by the same title with some of her English Language Learner reading students. Following that activity, the students dictated some new verses, which Dottie printed out on the computer. Each new verse was centered at the bottom of a single page for the students to illustrate and reread. One of the verses was, "This is the way we dance around, dance around, dance around." A few days later in a lesson with a new book, one of the girls, a preprimer reader in English, proudly recognized the word "dance" when she came across it in the text.

Another example comes from a story dictated by a child who attended the Literacy Development Center at the University of Nevada, Las Vegas to his tutor. Sammy is a second grader who was practically a "non-reader." He knew fewer than 20 sight words and possessed some knowledge of sound/symbol correspondence. He was able, according to his tutor, "to talk up a storm." Sammy and his tutor took a walk through the desert garden on campus. Then Sammy dictated the following:

> We walked to the desert garden today to see all the plants. I never knew there were so many different plants. I liked the teddy bear cactus the best. You have to be careful with cactus because it can stick you and then the sticker stays in your hand. Cactus don't need much water so that's why they grow so big in Las Vegas.

After the story was dictated, the tutor read the story to Sammy, had him echo read with her, and finally read it on his own. Once he seemed secure with the overall text, the tutor asked Sammy to find specific words from the story that were printed on 3 × 5 cards (see Figure 2.1).

The tutor selected these words for Sammy based on his previous sight word needs (e.g., "because") and for their interest for Sammy (e.g., "cactus"). A variety of activities were used to reinforce sight

FIGURE 2.1   Word Cards.

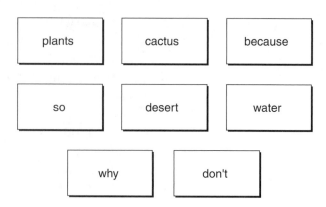

vocabulary: matching words on the card with words in the text; masking words in the text; and writing the words in Sammy's personal dictionary. The story was kept in Sammy's portfolio and used over several days.

Another word recognition lesson centered on /n/ as in *need, never,* and *knew.* What is special about *knew?* the tutor asked. This gave the tutor the opportunity to show Sammy the homophones *new* and *knew* and to help Sammy distinguish their use based on word meaning.

Teaching Aids

The best topics for LEA are based on actual experiences that children have had. Keep in mind that topics may come from daily life, school activities, or academic content. Figure 2.2 shows some suggested topics that may be used with groups or with individual children for language experience.

Daily Life	School Activities	Academic Content
Going Shopping	The Bus Ride to School	What happens
My New _____	Our Field Trip	when _____ is
My Pet _____	The Puppet Show	heated (cooled, etc.)
My Favorite TV Show	My Favorite Teacher	How to Add a Column of
		Numbers
		Our Favorite Author

FIGURE 2.2   Language Experience Approach Topics.

▰ READING THE ENVIRONMENT

Some struggling readers are unaware of the actual number of words they can read because they often see reading only as a school activity. The words around them in their community outside of school can be used to bolster their confidence and broaden their view of the place of reading in the real world. Teachers can assist struggling readers by bringing the children's world outside school into the classroom and thus help children to read the world around them and acknowledge the importance of non-school print.

The Power of the Strategy for Struggling Readers

Reading the environment helps struggling readers because it:

1. Demonstrates the use of print and its importance beyond the classroom.
2. Builds self-confidence because it shows struggling readers that they know many words even though they may not find the words in the classroom.
3. Provides second language learners with concrete examples.
4. Utilizes local resources.

Steps to Follow

1. Take students on a walking tour around the school neighborhood and have students write down any words or phrases that they see. If the walking tour is not possible, then take pictures of the community that include store signs, billboards, street signs.
2. Within the classroom, have the children make a replica of the community. They can make a mural or a model. Make word and phrase cards for labeling each item.
3. In small groups, have the children write about their community by incorporating the words and phrases into their text.
4. Have all children contribute to the making of a class community dictionary to keep track of new words.
5. Use community newspapers, flyers, and advertisements to expand word recognition.

Application and Example

The Paradise Professional Development School (PPDS) is located on the campus of the University of Nevada, Las Vegas right in the middle of a very urban area. It is not an affluent school by any means; over 70% of the children receive free or reduced lunches. In addition, 40% of the children have a language other than English as their first language.

Dottie is the remedial reading teacher for grades 3, 4, and 5 at the PPDS. She takes advantage of the school's location by taking her students on walking tours to read the environment. One place the children like to visit is the box office of the music hall. Students were given some 3 × 5 cards and a pencil. When they found words of interest

FIGURE 2.3 Words from a
Walking Tour to the Music Hall.

American Express Cards	Now open in the sidewalk cafe
One way	Do not enter
No Smoking	Box Office
Judy Bayley Theatre	Artemus W Ham Concert Hall
Department of Theatre Arts	Emergency Phone
Performing Arts Center Office	Automatic Door
Pull	Power Assist
Caution	KLVX TV Welcomes You
Before you write a check read this!	No Refunds
Stairs	Mastercard
VISA	The Canadian Brass
Tickets Now On Sale	Reserved Parking
Tow Away Zone	UNLV
No carts or vehicles beyond this point	Fire Lane
Burger King Express	Pizza Hut Express

to them or words they knew, the students were instructed to write them
down on the cards.

When they returned to Dottie's room the word cards were gathered
and compiled into a list, which Dottie made into a poster for the children
to see (Figure 2.3). After reading the words and phrases several times
together, the children began to suggest word categories. For example, the
children thought of one group as the "No Words"—"no smoking," "no
carts beyond this point," and "no refunds." Other words were related to
safety: "caution," "fire lane," "emergency phone."

Dottie encouraged the children to use some of the words and phrases
in their writing as well as to add to the list when they found words in the
community.

Teaching Aids

An example of the beginnings of a class community dictionary is
presented in Figure 2.4.

FIGURE 2.4 Classroom Community
Dictionary.

A –Apply within	E –
B –Bingo Sunday Night	F –Flamingo Avenue
	G –Grill and Restaurant
C –Community Center	H –Hospital Zone
D –Donuts	I –Interstate 95

■ DECODING BY ANALOGY

Balanced literacy instruction implies instruction in the three levels: comprehension, production, and metalinguistic awareness. Comprehension refers to the understanding of spoken or written language. Production is the creation of oral or written language. Metalinguistic awareness is an individual's ability to distance oneself from the comprehension and production of language and focus on the components of language itself. A child who is able to rhyme, spell, and edit is metalinguistically aware.

Metalinguistic awareness is the most abstract level of language and thus requires that children reach a level of abstract thinking. It is for this reason that young children in the primary grades may not be successful with some instructional practices, such as phonics. Unfortunately, many standardized reading tests for the early grades tend to question children on their abilities to manipulate language rather than the comprehension and production of it. Some children are labeled as remedial readers based on test results that require a level of thinking that all children do not reach at the same time.

The area of metalinguistic awareness that has received the most attention recently is phonemic awareness, the ability to understand that spoken language is made up of individual sounds—phonemes. A child who correctly answers the question, "With what sound does *bat* begin?" is phonemically aware. A child who produces a response such as "flies" or "ball" is trying to make sense of the question (comprehend) and is focused on the meaning of the word (i.e., a mammal that flies or a piece of sports equipment used to hit a ball). Responses such as these indicated that a child has not reached the phonemic awareness level and may not be developmentally ready for formal phonics instruction.

This then becomes the great dilemma for teachers: if children in my classroom have not entered into the metalinguistic/phonemic awareness stage of language development and yet they are tested on this, how can I help them become successful readers?

One way that is a successful strategy for struggling readers is based on the decoding by analogy (Cunningham, 1995). Gaskins, Ehri, O'Hare, and Donnelly (1997) described the success of this method, which is used at the Benchmark School, a school especially for children who struggle with reading. It is based on research of what mature readers do when they encounter an unknown word in text. Children learn to identify key phonograms (for example—*at;*—*ump;* and—*ight*) and then use what is known to decode the unknown.

The Power of the Strategy
for Struggling Readers

1. Decoding by analogy gives struggling readers a real boost because they can quickly increase their reading vocabulary.

2. The strategy allows the reader to focus on letter groups and their corresponding sound rather than a letter-by-letter/sound-by-sound decoding process.

3. Children learn to decode multisyllabic words easily once basic phonograms are learned.

Steps to Follow

1. This process assumes that children know the basic sound/symbol correspondence for consonants, blends, and digraphs.

2. Begin with a simple phonogram that is already found in a known sight word, such as "at" in cat.

3. Teach children this phrase, which will help them form the analogy: If this is—, then this must be—. For example, "if this is *cat*, then this must be *bat*," where cat is the known word and bat is the new word.

4. Post phonograms in the classroom on a bulletin board or "word wall" for a quick reference when children are reading and writing.

5. Find authentic texts for children to use to practice their skills in decoding by analogy. Avoid texts that overuse phonograms, however, so that children apply their skill in real reading situations. Text such as "The fat cat sat on a mat" are of no real value to children.

Application and Example

Brandon is a third grader who attended the Literacy Development Center for tutoring. His oral reading was very laborious; he seemed to be very confused when confronted with words that were multisyllabic and broke down to a letter-by-letter decoding. He also is very reluctant to try new words. He was aware of the fact that he was falling behind his classmates in school. During the initial interview, Brandon told his tutor Steve that he wanted to learn how to read "really big words."

Results from initial assessments showed that Brandon knew most high-frequency words, initial and final consonant sounds, two letter blends, and short vowels. Steve decided to try to help Brandon apply what he already knew to decode unfamiliar words.

Steve: There are lots of ways to figure out big words. I'm going to show you a way that you can use because you already know many things about words. Let's look at this word: LIGAMENT. Do you know what it is?

Brandon: No.

Steve:	Okay, if we look at the first three letters, LIG. The L is a consonant, the I is a vowel, and the G is a consonant. Do you know another word that looks like LIG that has a different first consonant but the same I and G? It would look like ____IG.
Brandon:	No.
Steve:	Sure you do. What about B-I-G?
Brandon:	That's "big."
Steve:	And P-I-G?
Brandon:	That's "pig."
Steve:	So how would you say L-I-G?
Brandon:	"Lig."
Steve:	Okay, so the first part of the word is LIG and we know that because we know similar words like "big" and "pig." Now let's look at the rest of the word: A-MENT. I'm going to tell you that the "A" is a short *a* sound, so now we have LIG-A. Look at the last part MENT. Do you know any word that looks like that—that has a different first consonant instead of the *M* but the same other letters ENT?
Brandon:	I know "went."
Steve:	Great! So if W-E-N-T is WENT then. M-E-N-T is. . . .
Brandon:	MENT
Steve:	Right. Now let's put it all together.
Brandon:	LIG- A- MENT.
Steve:	And if we say it fast it's LIGAMENT. Do you know what a ligament is?
Brandon:	No.
Steve:	Let's read this sentence with the word and see if you can tell what it means.
Brandon:	"The football player tore a ligament in his leg."
Steve:	What do you think a ligament is?
Brandon:	Is it a muscle?
Steve:	Yes, it is part of our body that connects muscles. If you tear a ligament, it can be very painful. Now, let's see if you can try another word using this strategy.

Teaching Aids

Figure 2.5 provides a list of common phonograms. Teachers should keep in mind that this list is presented as a teaching reference and is not intended to be reproduced for children to memorize or use without context.

FIGURE 2.5 Common Phonograms with Example Words.

am	clam, ham, jam, ram, tam, yam, Sam
ast	blast, cast, fast, last, mast, past, vast
ack	back, black, hack, jack, lack, sack
ar	bar, car, far, mar, scar, tar
at	bat, cat, fat, flat, pat, sat, that, vat
ate	bate, crate, date, rate, gate, grate, late, plate, rate, skate, state
aw	claw, draw, flaw, jaw, law, paw, raw, saw
eal	deal, meal, peal, real, seal, steal, veal
ean	bean, clean, dean, lean, mean
eat	beat, cleat, feat, meat, neat, seat, treat
ed	bed, bled, fled, led, pled, shed, sled, red, wed
eep	beep, cheep, creep, deep, jeep, keep, peep, sheep, sweep, weep
in	bin, chin, fin, pin, shin, tin, win
ing	bring, cling, fling, King, ring, sing, string, swing, thing
it	bit, fit, hit, kit, pit, skit, wit
ive	dive, drive, five, hive, live
ob	bob, cob, job, mob, rob, slob, sob
old	bold, cold, fold, gold, mold, sold, told
op	cop, chop, crop, drop, flop, hop, mop, pop, shop, stop, top
ope	cope, dope, hope, mope, pope, slope
ox	box, fox, lox, pox, sox
ump	bump, dump, grump, jump, lump, pump, slump, thump
un	bun, fun, gun, nun, pun, stun, sun
ust	bust, crust, dust, gust, just, must, rust, trust

■ SIGHT WORD DEVELOPMENT—SEMANTIC ORGANIZERS

A major goal of literacy instruction is for students to read with a high level of fluency so they can identify individual words and phrases used by an author with such rapidity that they can concentrate fully on the meaning of a text rather than using an inordinate amount of mental energy decoding words. We want decoding to become automatic (Samuels, Schermer, & Reinking, 1992) and the act of reading always meaningful. The larger the number of words readers recognize instantly, the more rapidly text is decoded and, thus, the more fluent the readers.

Remedial and classroom teachers are, however, well aware of children who have a large number of words in their sight vocabularies, who read orally with great fluency but who do not comprehend the text. These children have been identified as "word callers." They often are very successful readers in the early grades because the complexity of the text's meaning is minimal. It is the word callers who often are referred to remedial reading classes because they "just don't understand a thing they read." These word callers are often heralded by their parents as being able to read "any book you hand them." Teachers must help children and parents understand that reading is a meaning-making activity; without meaning children are not reading.

A distinction may be made between sight vocabularies and sight words. All words have the potential of becoming part of an individual's sight vocabulary; mature avid readers have enormous sight vocabularies. Sight vocabularies also become specialized as readers enter into various fields of study. A word such as *pryazinamide* most likely is a sight word for physicians and pharmacists but not for the general public. By the way, pryazinamide is a drug used to treat tuberculosis.

Sight words are "a relatively small set of words in our language that do not conform to rules of pronunciation or analytical techniques learned by children beginning to read" (Gipe, 1995, p. 183). Included here are high-frequency words, which make up between 50% to 65% of all words in written text. The word lists complied by Dolch (1935) and Fry, et. al. (1993) are examples of sight word lists that have been used by classroom teachers over the years as teaching references and study lists for children. These high-frequency, nonphonetic words are often the very words that cause some children to struggle with both reading and writing.

With this in mind, children do need to learn sight words and to continually add to their sight vocabularies throughout their years in school and beyond. Providing opportunities for children to read and reread books, poetry, and other text is perhaps the way for children to learn sight words. However, this may not be enough for some children.

Pehrsson and Robinson (1985) presented the semantic organizer approach to writing and reading instruction. This approach has many purposes for literacy instruction; one is improving sight vocabulary in a contextual setting.

Power of the Strategy for Struggling Readers

1. Children have multiple exposure to sight words within a known context.
2. Children build their mental organizations or schema for words, which aids in recall.
3. Children use sight words in reading and writing.
4. Children learn indirectly how language functions in terms of parts of speech.

Steps to Follow

1. Collect a variety of pictures of objects, animals, and people that children can easily identify. Photographs from magazines as well as computer clip art work well. Paste the pictures on 3 × 5 cards, print the picture names, and laminate.
2. Select three pictures of items that share an attribute that can be expressed in a single word and one picture of an item that doesn't have that attribute. For example, Figure 2.6 shows three different birds that fly and a dog that doesn't.
3. Show children the picture word cards and present other sight words that will allow them to create simple sentences orally.

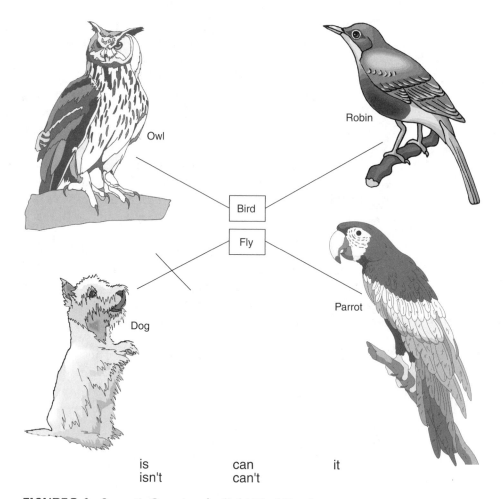

FIGURE 2.6   Semantic Organizer for Sight Word Development.

4. Help children "read" the semantic organizer by clarifying that the single line means the presence of an attribute while the crossed line means the attribute is missing.

5. Either as a group or individually, have the children write the sentences generated by the semantic organizer.

Application and Example

Mrs. Elwood's second-grade class was studying living things. Several of the children were having difficulties with basic sight words. Mrs. Elwood brought those children together in a group to continue their understanding of living things and to reinforce sight word recognition.

After sharing the picture words (*owl, robin, parrot, dog*) and the functional sight words (*fly, bird, can, can't, is, isn't, it*), the children created the following text:

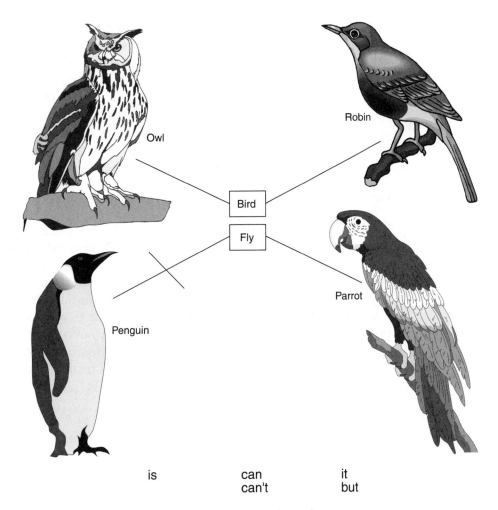

FIGURE 2.7 Semantic Organizer for Sight Word Development.

An owl is a bird. It can fly. A robin is a bird.
It can fly. A parrot is a bird. It can fly.
A dog isn't a bird. It can't fly.

A few days later, Mrs. Elwood reviewed with children the paragraph they had written earlier and then introduced the semantic organizer shown in Figure 2.7. She focused the children's attention on the change from *dog* to *penguin* and the sight word *but*.

After a science discussion on penguins, the children stated and then wrote the following:

An owl is a bird. It can fly. A robin is a bird.
It can fly. A parrot is a bird. It can fly.
A penguin is a bird but it can't fly.

The children were encouraged to reread their paragraph for sight word reinforcement. Finally, the children were asked to think of how "and" could be used in their paragraph, which resulted in:

> An owl is a bird and it can fly. A robin is a bird and it can fly. A parrot is a bird and it can fly. A penguin is a bird but it can't fly.

■ SIGHT WORD DEVELOPMENT—CLOZE ACTIVITIES

The high-frequency, nonphonetic words that often cause readers great difficulty can become more friendly if children understand that these words are a natural part of our oral language and that many of these words are very predictable if the readers read with meaning in mind.

Taylor (1953) presented the cloze procedure as a method for determining text readability. His work is based on the psychological phenomena that the human mind wants always to have things completed, the sense of closure. For example, if you saw the following, your mind wants to complete the drawing and form a triangle.

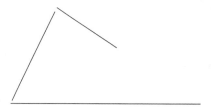

In relationship to reading and language, our mind works the same way and wants to complete the sentence or phrase read or uttered. Think about how often it has happened that you are able to complete your friend's or mate's sentence before he or she does. We are able to do this because we share the same context and because our language is both redundant and predictable.

Goodman's work also provides insight into the connection between language and reading (1968). He defined reading as a "psycholinguistic guessing game." Goodman suggested that because of our understanding of oral language, we can easily predict or guess what the next word will be in oral and written text. While all literacy educators and researchers may not agree with this definition, it does assist teachers as they work with struggling readers. For example, in the sentence, "I like to eat_____ ," there are many possible answers but not an infinite number because language pattern words already used start to limit the possible guesses. Responses from children such as *bananas* or *peaches* indicate that for the child (1) language is meaning based and (2) that comprehension is occurring. The number of responses is further limited when children focus on the graphophonemes present in the word when the missing word is provided: "I like to eat *popcorn.*" Now, given the responses *bananas* and *peaches*, *peaches* is the better choice. The guess is still incorrect, however. If the sentence is in isolation, then readers must rely on their decoding knowledge because they do not know it by sight. If, as is usually the case for authentic written text, more context is provided either before or after the unknown word, readers can more accurately predict the correct response. "I like to eat *popcorn*. I enjoy it at the movies." Because of a shared language and social experiences, the missing word has to be popcorn.

The cloze procedure utilizes this knowledge of language and society. Taylor's procedure originally focused on using cloze as a way to determine the readability of a text in terms of how well a reader and author were matched. The cloze procedure is also a valuable tool through which struggling readers can learn sight words and develop their sight vocabularies.

The Power of the Strategy for Struggling Readers

1. Children use their knowledge of oral language to help them read unknown written words. It is especially helpful for second-language learners.
2. Children continue to reinforce their understanding that reading is a meaning-making activity.
3. Children build their self-confidence and are willing to take risks to predict unknown words.

Steps to Follow

1. Building from Oral Language—Depending on the oral language abilities of the children, the teacher may begin with picture word cards. For example, show children related pairs of words such as *boy/girl, dog/cat, in/out,* and *up/down.* Have them listen to sentences and supply the missing words:

   The dog ran up the stairs so the cat ran _____ the stairs.
   The boy chased the girl in and _____ of the door.

2. Do the same exercises with written text. Discuss how the structure of the sentence helps to make the prediction of the missing word more accurate.
3. Expand the amount of text and have the children read along as you read and think out loud to model the thought process. The text in Figure 2.8 is taken from *I Like to be Little* by Charlotte Zolotow (Harper & Row, 1987).
4. First read the passage completely, saying *blank* for the missing words. Tell the children that the author leaves clues in the sentences so that

Once there was a little _____ .

"What do you want to be when you grow _____ ?" her mother asked.

"I just want to stay _____ right now," she said.

"Why?" said her _____ . "It's nice to be grown _____ ? Why do you want to be little?"

"Because I am," said the little girl, "and _____ when you are little you can do things you _____ do when you grow up."

FIGURE 2.8   Cloze Text to Improve Sight Word Development.

you can predict missing words correctly. Then begin to model your thought process. For example:

"There is a blank in the first sentence but the author helps me by using the word *her* in the second sentence. I also know that two people are talking to each other because I see quotation marks. One person is the mother. The missing word in the first sentence most likely is *girl.*

5. Continue in like manner, gradually having the children take over the think aloud.
6. Have children work with a partner on a similar passage that reinforces some of the same sight words. Provide them with several opportunities to practice the strategy.
7. Provide excerpts from other children's books in which the author provides the reader with enough support to make predictions. Have the children write their prediction in the blank, then check the original text for accuracy.

Application and Example

A variation on cloze is maze. It may be easier for some children to begin with this because choices are presented to help with readers. For each

Once there was a little _____ (boy, girl, out).

"What do you want to be when you grow

_____ ?" (fire, down, up) her mother asked.

"I just want to stay _____ (little, big, water)

right now," she said.

FIGURE 2.9   A Maze Passage.

of the missing words, three word choices are provided in random order: a word from the same part of speech; the correct response; and a word that isn't meaningful in the text.

Joy, a tutor at the Literacy Development Center, decided to use the maze strategy prior to using cloze with Alicia, a second grader who was having difficulty with sight words. Joy first read *I Like to be Little* (Zolotow, 1987) in its entirety to Alicia as she followed along. After discussing the story, Joy showed Alicia the text in Figure 2.9 written on a lapboard. Using a think-aloud procedure similar to the one for cloze, Joy helped Alicia decide which words were the best choices.

Joy prepared a second passage for Alicia to write on as she considered the choices for the missing word. To keep Alicia thinking about the importance of making meaning when reading, she would ask questions such as:

"Why did you pick that word?"

"Does that word make sense for you?"

"What clues in the sentence did you use to help you?"

Once Alicia had completed the exercise, Joy gave her the book so Alicia could check her own responses with the real text.

Teaching Aids

Figure 2.10 presents Fry's list of 300 words that most educators would agree are essential for readers to know instantly.

First Hundred

the	or	will	number	he	we	some	call	at	she
of	one	no	had	was	when	her	who	two	get
up	and	other	by	for	your	would	oil	be	do
about	way	could	to	on	can	make	its	more	come
a	word	out	people	are	said	like	now	this	how
in	but	many	my	as	there	him	find	write	made
is	not	then	than	with	use	into	long	have	their
you	what	them	first	his	an	time	down	go	may
that	all	these	water	they	each	has	day	from	if
it	were	so	been	I	which	look	dig	see	part

Second Hundred

over	say	set	try	live	mean	such	away	name	also
new	great	put	kind	me	old	because	animal	land	still
sound	where	end	hand	back	any	turn	house	good	around
take	help	does	picture	give	same	here	point	different	learn
only	through	another	again	most	tell	why	page	sentence	form
little	much	well	change	very	boy	ask	letter	home	should
work	before	large	off	after	follow	went	mother	man	three
know	line	must	play	thing	came	men	answer	us	America
place	right	big	spell	our	want	read	found	think	small
year	too	even	air	just	show	need	study	move	world

Third Hundred

high	saw	important	miss	last	next	sea	let	light	together
every	left	until	idea	school	hard	began	above	hear	song
near	don't	children	enough	father	open	grow	girl	thought	got
add	few	side	cat	keep	example	took	sometimes	stop	being
food	while	feet	face	tree	begin	river	mountain	head	group
between	along	car	watch	never	filed	four	cut	without	leave
own	might	mile	far	start	always	carry	young	under	often
below	close	night	Indian	city	those	state	talk	second	family
country	something	walk	really	earth	both	once	soon	story	run
plant	seem	white	almost	eye	paper	book	list	later	it's

Common suffixes: -*s*, -*ing*, -*ed*, -*er*, -ly, -est

FIGURE 2.10   Fry's First 300 Instant Words. From: *Reading Teachers Book of Lists*. 3rd Edition by Edward Fry, Jacqueline Kress, Dona Lee Fountoukidis. Copyright © 1993. Reprinted with permission of Learning Network Direct, a part of the Learning Network.

■ VOCABULARY DEVELOPMENT— MULTIPLE-MEANING WORDS

How many definitions can you think of for the word *run?* Let's see:

Moving very fast

A run in my stockings

A dog run

Running for the presidency

The refrigerator is running

All of these definitions are possible as well as all those listed in Figure 2.11.

run (run), *v.*, **ran, run, run·ning**, *n., adj.* —*v.i.* **1.** to go quickly by moving the legs more rapidly than at a walk and in such a manner that for an instant in each step all or both feet are off the ground. **2.** to move with haste; act quickly: *Run upstairs and get the iodine.* **3.** to depart quickly; take to flight; flee or escape: *to run from danger.* **4.** to have recourse for aid, support, comfort, etc.: *He shouldn't run to his parents with every little problem.* **5.** to make a quick trip or informal visit for a short stay at a place: *to run up to New York; I will run over to see you after dinner.* **6.** to go around, rove, or ramble without restraint (often fol. by *about*): *to run about in the park.* **7.** to move, roll, or progress from momentum or from being hurled, kicked, or otherwise propelled: *The wheel ran over the curb and into the street.* **8.** *Sports.* **a.** to take part in a race or contest. **b.** to finish in a race or contest in a certain numerical position: *The horse ran second.* **9.** to be or campaign as a candidate for election. **10.** to migrate, as fish: *to run in huge shoals.* **11.** to migrate upstream or inshore from deep water to spawn. **12.** to move under continuing power or force, as of the wind, a motor, etc.: *The car ran along the highway.* **13.** (of a ship, automobile, etc.) to be sailed or driven from a safe, proper, or given route: *The ship ran aground.* **14.** to ply between places, as a vessel or conveyance: *This bus runs between New Haven and Hartford.* **15.** to move, glide, turn, rotate, or pass easily, freely, or smoothly: *A rope runs in a pulley.* **16.** to creep, trail, or climb, as growing vines: *The ivy ran up the side of the house.* **17.** to come undone or to unravel, as stitches or a fabric: *these stockings run easily.* **18.** to flow, as a liquid: *Let the water run before you drink it.* **19.** to flow along, esp. strongly, as a stream or the sea: *The rapids ran over the rocks.* **20.** to empty or transfer contents: *The river ran into the sea.* **21.** to appear, occur, or exist within a certain limited range; include a specific range of variations (usually fol. by *from*): *Your work runs from fair to bad.* **22.** to melt and flow or drip: *Wax ran down the burning candle.* **23.** *Golf.* (of a golf ball) to bounce or roll along the ground just after landing from a stroke: *The ball struck the green and ran seven feet past the hole.* **24.** to spread on being applied to a surface, as a liquid: *Fresh paint ran over the window molding onto the pane.* **25.** to spread over a material when exposed to moisture: *The dyes in this fabric are* guaranteed not to run in washing. **26.** to undergo a spreading of colors: *materials that run when washed.* **27.** to flow forth as a discharge: *Tears ran from her eyes.* **28.** to discharge or give passage to a liquid or fluid: *Her eyes ran with tears.* **29.** to operate or function: *How does your new watch run? Cars run on gasoline.* **30.** to be in operation: *the noise of a dishwasher running.* **31.** to continue in operation: *The furnace runs most of the day.* **32.** to elapse; pass or go by, as time: *Time is running out, and we must hurry.* **33.** to pass into or meet with a certain state or condition: *to run into debt; to run into trouble.* **34.** to get or become: *The well ran dry.* **35.** to amount; total: *The bill ran to $100.* **36.** to be stated or worded in a certain manner: *The minutes of the last meeting run as follows.* **37.** *Com.* **a.** to accumulate, follow, or become payable in due course, as interest on a debt: *Your interest runs from January 1st to December 31st.* **b.** to make many withdrawals in rapid succession, as from a bank. **38.** *Law.* **a.** to have legal force or effect, as a writ. **b.** to continue to operate. **c.** to go along with: *The easement runs with the land.* **39.** to proceed, continue, or go: *The story runs for eight pages.* **40.** to extend in a given direction: *This road runs north to Litchfield.* **41.** to extend for a certain length: *The unpaved section runs for eight miles.* **42.** to extend over a given surface: *Shelves ran from floor to ceiling.* **43.** to be printed, as on a printing press: *Two thousand copies ran before the typo was caught.* **44.** to appear in print or be published as a story, photograph, etc., in a newspaper, magazine, or the like: *The account ran in all the papers. The political cartoon always runs on the editorial page.* **45.** to be performed on a stage or be played continually, as a play: *The play ran for two years.* **46.** to occur or take place continuously, as a movie: *The picture runs for two hours.* **47.** to pass quickly: *A thought ran through his mind. Her eyes ran over the room.* **48.** to be disseminated, circulated, or spread rapidly: *The news of his promotion ran all over town.* **49.** to continue or return persistently; recur: *The old tune ran through his mind all day.* **50.** to have or tend to have or produce a specified character, quality, form, etc.: *This novel runs to long descriptions. Her sister is fat too, but the family runs to being overweight.* **51.** to be or continue to be of a certain or average size, number, etc.: *Potatoes are running large this year.* **52.** *Naut.* to sail before the wind. —*v.t.* **53.** to move or run along (a surface, way, path, etc.): *Every morning he ran the dirt path around the reservoir to keep in condition. She ran her fingers over the*

FIGURE 2.11 Definitions for the Word "Run." The *Random House Webster's Unabridged Dictionary* (1998) lists more than 125 definitions and contextual meanings for the word run.

Good readers know that the appropriate definition for the word *run* depends on the context in which it is used. Struggling readers may be very able to decode the word and know its meaning in one context, but cannot comprehend a text that uses a different meaning for the word. Meyerson, Ford, & Jones (1991) showed how third and fifth graders can easily apply the wrong definition to known words even when given the context for the definition. Thus, building sight vocabulary also implies an understanding of which meaning fits the given context.

Teachers are often puzzled by young readers who decode multiple meaning words correctly but who fail to comprehend what they've read. Wide reading in many different types of text will aid many struggling readers to learn new meanings for known words; for others, more direct instruction may be needed. Teachers should also keep in mind that there is a developmental aspect to learning new meanings for known words as documented in *The Living Vocabulary* (Dale & O'Rourke, 1979).

The Power of the Strategy for Struggling Readers

1. Students already recognize the word, so decoding isn't a problem.
2. Most of the common multiple-meaning words are words in students' oral language if their first language is English. Multiple-meaning words often cause confusion for second-language learners and require many exposures in meaningful text.
3. Students' awareness that reading and writing are meaning-making thought processes is heightened.

Steps to Follow

1. Select three to five words to be taught in one lesson.
2. Present the words on the board or overhead. Give the students the same words on cards (see Figure 2.12 for examples).
3. Use one of the words in a written sentence and ask the students to provide a meaning for the word. For example:

   A. My mother asked me to *set* the table before dinner.
4. After the students have agreed on a definition, present a new sentence.

   B. Jamie was always 10 minutes late for school, so his mother _____ the clock ahead 10 minutes.
5. Ask the students to hold up the word that best fits the sentence from the cards they have.
6. Discuss how *set* is also the correct answer in sentence B and A. What definition can you give for *set* in sentence B? How is the meaning different for the word *set* in the two sentences?
7. Ask the students if they can think of another definition for *set* or how they have heard people use the word in a different way. They may suggest *set*, as in "set the book on the table," or *set*, as in "ready, set, go."
8. Repeat the steps for the other words for the lesson.

FIGURE 2.12 Some Common High-frequency Multiple-meaning Words.

about	run	spell	can
will	down	mean	right
page	letter	head	saw
state	hard	above	band
back	set	well	have
head	bank	high	on
by	use	book	face
miss	side	light	last
point	left	take	off
over	home	get	cut

Application and Example

Dottie's second graders who attend the reading improvement program were having fun listening to Dottie read *Amelia Bedelia* books. After sharing several with them, Dottie selected the word *light* for the second graders to explore for multiple meanings:

Turn off the *light*

Light the candle

The baby doesn't weigh much; she is *light* as a feather

Light toast, not dark

The dawn's early *light*

A *light* touch

Dottie then asked the children to illustrate a correct meaning of light and the way Amelia Bedelia would interpret it. Rico's picture appears in Figure 2.13.

FIGURE 2.13   Illustration of Multiple Meanings for the Word "Light."

PROFESSIONAL REFERENCES FOR IMPROVING WORD RECOGNITION

Allen, R. V. (1976). *Language experiences in communication.* Boston: Houghton Mifflin.

Barr, R. & Johnson, B. (1997). *Teaching reading and writing in the elementary classroom.* New York: Longman.

Cunningham, P. (1995). *Phonics they use: Words for reading and writing.* New York: Harper Collins.

Dale, E. & O'Rourke, J. (1979). *The Living Vocabulary.* Palo Alto, CA: Field Educational Publications.

Dolch, E. (1953). *Dolch basic sight vocabulary.* Champaign, IL: Garrard.

Fry, E. B., Kress, J., & Fountoukidis, D. (1993). *The Reading Teachers' Book of List* 3/e. Englewood Cliffs, NJ: Prentice Hall.

Gaskins, I., Ehri, L., O'Hare, C., & Donnelly, K. (1997). Procedures for word learning: Making discoveries about words. *The Reading Teacher, 50,* 312–327.

Gipe, J. (1995). *Corrective reading techniques for the classroom teacher.* Scottsdale, AZ: Gorsuch Scarisbrick Publishers.

Goodman, K. (1968). The psycholinguistic nature of the reading process. In K. S. Goodman (Ed.). *The psycholinguistic nature of the reading process.* Detroit: Wayne State Press.

Hall, M. (1978). *The language experience approach for teaching reading: A research perspective.* Newark, DE: International Reading Association.

Meyerson, M. J., Ford, M. S., & Jones, W. P. (1991). Science vocabulary knowledge of third and fifth grade students. *Science Education, 74* (4), 419–428.

Newman, F. & Holzman, L. (1993). *Lev Vygotsky: Revolutionary scientist.* London: Routledge.

Pehrsson, R. & Robinson, H. A. (1985). *The semantic organizer approach to reading and writing.* Rockville, MD: Aspen Publications.

Samuels, S., Schermer N., & Reinking, D. (1992). Reading fluency: Techniques for making decoding automatic. In S. Samuels & A. Farstrup (Eds.), *What research has to say about reading instruction* (pp. 124–144). Newark, DE: International Reading Association.

Taylor, W. (1953). Cloze procedure: A new tool for measuring readability. *Journalism Quarterly, 30* 415–433.

■ PART ■ III

When Struggling Readers Need to Improve Comprehension

There are times when even the best readers have difficulty understanding a text. Comprehension difficulties arise for many reasons; some may be considered a mismatch between author and reader. A reader may fail to understand a given text because the author (1) uses unfamiliar vocabulary and/or complex sentence structures, and (2) discusses topics or ideas for which the reader has no prior knowledge or experiences. Other factors such as reader interest also affect comprehension.

Some youngsters do well in reading until they begin to read more content area materials such as in science and social studies texts. These children are very comfortable with narrative text, but they are unfamiliar with the overall structure of expository text. Many opportunities to read a variety of text as well as some direct instruction about the structure of expository text are ways in which children can improve their comprehension.

For other children, comprehension difficulties are more specific. The difficulties may stem from a child's lack of understanding of what reading is all about: without meaning there is no reading. Other comprehension problems may be seen when children are asked to think critically or to make inferences about the text. In both instances, direct instruction and modeling are appropriate teaching methods.

■ RETELLING

Retelling, often written about in terms of an assessment tool (Gambrell, Pfeiffer, & Wilson, 1985; Morrow, 1988; Tierney, Readence, & Dishner, 1995), can be used as a strategy to enhance the comprehension of struggling readers. When the reading of the selection is finished, the student is expected to retell the story, as if to a friend who has never heard it before. Information from the text, combined with personal meaning, is repeated and rehearsed during reading, as the student prepares for the oral retelling. Concentrating on the story elements leads to a more in-depth understanding of the text. Practice in retelling contributes to improved comprehension in both proficient and less-proficient readers (Gambrell, Koskinen, & Kapinus, 1991).

Steps to Follow

1. Retelling can first be modeled by the teacher. Read aloud a story, stopping from time to time, to plan aloud what information will be included in the retelling. When the reading of the selection is finished, retell it.
2. Before reading, tell the student to be prepared to retell the story after the selection has been read. The student should tell it as if to a friend who has never heard it before.
3. Tell the student what is expected in the retelling of the story: characters, setting, plot with main episodes, and resolution.
4. Have the student read and retell the story.
5. The student can be allowed the use of puppets, story boards, or other props during the retelling.
6. If the student is having difficulty retelling the story, the teacher can prompt with questions: What happened in the beginning? Where did the story take place? What happened next? How was the problem solved? How did the story end?
7. If important details of the story have been omitted in the retelling, the teacher can ask specific questions or refer the student back to the text to reread excluded sections.

Applications and Examples

Retelling is a strategy that can be used with students in all grade levels. Students can retell a story one-on-one with the teacher, with a peer partner, or in a small group. Retelling can be used across the curriculum with both fiction and nonfiction books.

It can be further extended by using a variety of story guides for fiction and a variety of graphic organizers for nonfiction. Two examples of story guides often used in elementary classrooms are made with a 12 × 18 sheet of white construction paper.

1. Beginning, middle, and end (see Figure 3.1A).
   The piece of construction paper is folded lengthwise. Only on the front piece, two slits are made from the edge to the fold, creating three equal sections. These are labeled: Beginning, Middle, and End. Opening up the construction paper story guide, the student then writes a brief sentence and draws an illustration for each labeled part of the story.
2. Characters, setting, plot, and solution (see Figure 3.1B).
   The piece of construction paper is folded lengthwise. Only on the front piece, three slits are made from the edge to the fold, creating

FIGURE 3.1A   Retelling Story
Guide.

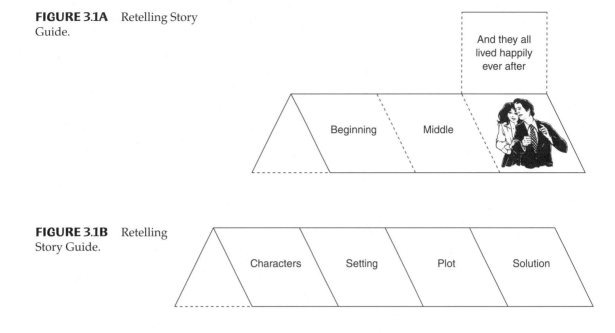

FIGURE 3.1B   Retelling
Story Guide.

four equal sections. These are labeled Characters, Setting, Plot, and
Solution. Opening up the construction paper story guide, the student
then writes a brief sentence and draws an illustration for each labeled
part of the story.

■ UNDERSTANDING TEXT STRUCTURE

Authors of expository text write differently than authors of narrative text
in the way they organize their thoughts and communicate information to
their readers. Expository text explains and informs the reader about
topics, concepts, and ideas. Often these topics, concepts, and ideas are
foreign to readers. This, coupled with the fact that expository text
structure differs from narrative, makes expository text challenging for
many students. Teachers can help their students understand expository
text structure through direct instruction of text structures. Common text
structures include enumeration, time order, compare/contrast,
cause/effect, and problem/solution (Vacca & Vacca, 1986).

The Power of the Strategy
for Struggling Readers

By helping struggling readers understand the different text structures
used by authors we:

1. Provide them with a way to understand the author's message through
   an understanding of how language is organized in a text.
2. Introduce key vocabulary words and phrases that help readers
   recognize the text structure and predict what will be next in the text.

For example, "on the other hand" is a key phrase used by authors when comparing and contrasting topics, concepts, or ideas.

3. Assist students with their own writing as they learn more about what authors do with expository text. They learn how to read like a writer (Smith, 1983).

Steps to Follow

1. Select two common objects that are familiar to all children in your class or group (e.g., an apple and an orange).
2. Draw two overlapping circles (Venn Diagram) on the board or overhead projector.
3. Ask the children to brainstorm the characteristics of each object and list them on the areas of the circles that do not overlap.
4. Then ask the children to read the characteristics that both objects have in common. Write these in the overlapping area.
5. Present a short paragraph to the children that compares and contrasts the two objects. Read the paragraph to them and model using a "think-aloud" exercise on how to understand the text. Point out key words and phrases that signal the compare/contrast text structure.
6. Have the children look through science and social studies books to see if they can locate paragraphs in which the author uses the compare/contrast structure.
7. Ask the children to write about two objects of their choice in which they use the compare/contrast structure.
8. Working with a partner, have the children identify key words and phrases in their partners' paragraphs.

Application and Examples

In Mary Ann's sixth grade class, students were having difficulties with their new social studies textbook. They seldom read their assignments and consistently did poorly on exams. However, they were able to read novels at their grade level.

Mary Ann did a readability check on the text and found that it ranged from fifth to eighth grade. Upon closer examination, she noticed that the authors often used the cause/effect and problem/solution text pattern in their writing. She decided to give her class a series of mini-lessons on these text patterns and the key or signal words found in the text.

One lesson involved the students in writing paragraphs about topics of their interest. In the paragraph they had to use signal words that helped the reader understand the word *because*. Scott wrote the following:

> Lake Mead can be a fun place to play since it isn't polluted. Because almost no chemicals come into the lake, there is a plentiful supply of fish and very little algae. There are strict laws and high fines for dumping. As a result, people can enjoy the lake for recreation.

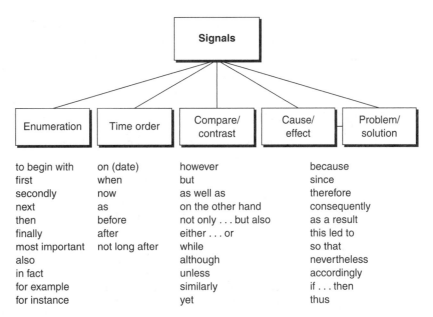

FIGURE 3.2 Signal Words for Expository Text. *Content Area Reading,* 3rd ed. by Richard T. Vacca and Jo Anne L. Vacca. Copyright © 1989, 1986 by Richard T. Vacca and Jo Anne L. Vacca. Reprinted by permission of Addison-Wesley Educational Publishers, Inc.

Teaching Aids

Once children begin to read expository text, explicit instruction in its text patterns will assist their understanding of the text. Children can recognize and anticipate signal words that authors use in their writing. This will in turn enhance their comprehension and production of text.

■ CONCEPT-ORIENTED READING INSTRUCTION

Concept-Oriented Reading Instruction (CORI) is organized around a broad conceptual theme that integrates science and language arts (Guthrie & McCann, 1997). CORI consists of the following instructional characteristics: conceptual theme, observation, self-direction, strategies, collaboration, self-expression, and coherence. This strategy helps struggling readers to better understand the text they read as well as increase student motivation to engage in literacy activities.

The Power of the Strategy for Struggling Readers

1. The social component allows for students to engage in a cooperative learning process where their thoughts and the thoughts of their peers can intermingle to clarify points and improve comprehension.
2. By capitalizing on students' interest in a topic, the teacher can help them make mental connections to prior knowledge and stimulate their curiosity and openness to new ideas.

3. Struggling readers are provided with concrete examples that can be used to build more abstract thinking and understand complex text.

Steps to Follow

1. *Conceptual theme:* Select a broad conceptual theme from the science curriculum; for example, life cycles.
2. *Observation:* Provide a real-life experience with concrete objects, while teaching and modeling strategies for observation. This step leads to student questioning and motivation. Allow time for discussions and journal reflections.
3. *Self-direction:* Provide a framework with choices of topics, tasks, and media for learning. Provide scaffolding, resources, and goals for activities. Students take responsibility for their own learning by making choices.
4. *Strategies:* Serve as a coach, engaging students through modeling, peer tutoring, and whole-class discussions on selection and use of strategies. The emphasized strategies are problem finding, using prior knowledge, searching for information, comprehending informational text, self-monitoring, and interpreting literary text.
5. *Collaboration:* Provide for social structures that include not only individual work but also small groups or teams, partnerships, and whole group activities. Provide support for collaborative work by assisting and monitoring students listening to others, respecting perspectives, and using information from each other.
6. *Self-expression:* Allow students to select the topic or style of communication. Students may choose to create posters, make videos, write, or perform.
7. *Coherence:* Coherence is inherent to the CORI instructional framework, as students participate in the activities that link real-life experiences to conceptual understanding.

Application and Examples

Using life cycles as a broad conceptual theme, introduce plants with a real-life experience with seeds. Provide a variety of fruits and vegetables for the students to investigate. They can begin by predicting and estimating the size and number of seeds. As the items are cut up and seeds are examined, many questions will be raised. Provide the students with a wide variety of children's literature that lends itself to the investigation of seeds and plants. Include all genres; some students may want to read contemporary realistic fiction, folk tales, legends, or science fiction about plants as they become immersed in the topic. Assist students in acquiring access to other media to investigate plant life.

▥ BREAKING DOWN THE TEXT

When children are exposed to good literature as part of their literacy development, they are introduced to authors who use real language in real ways. The texts tell engaging stories or present interesting facts written with sentence structure that may be very different from children's own speech patterns as well as the structure used in early basal readers or leveled books. Through the oral reading of good literature to children, teachers develop children's listening comprehension of texts with complex sentence structures and less common language patterns. As listeners, children are often drawn to these texts just because of the novel language patterns used by the authors. These texts may challenge readers to make sense of the author's message and require modeling and explanation from skilled teachers. "Breaking down the text" is a strategy through which teachers can show children how to make complex text more simple and understandable.

The Power of the Strategy for Struggling Readers

1. The strategy leads to independence in reading comprehension because it allows them to understand how complex and lengthy sentences can be broken down into more manageable parts.
2. Children learn to understand an author's style of writing.
3. The strategy may help children write more complex sentences in their own compositions.

Steps to Follow

1. Select a paragraph from a children's book, textbook, or newspaper in which the author uses complex sentence structures and a variety of punctuation. Text that is at a small group's "too hard" level is appropriate.
2. Reproduce the paragraph for the children. Leave spacing between lines of print so words and phrases can be underlined, circled, etc.
3. Work on the overhead projector with the text while the children follow along on their individual copies.
4. Read the selection to the children. Ask the students to follow along and be ready to find sentences, words, and punctuation.
5. Following the teacher's model, have the students number the sentences.
6. Through modeling and questioning, help the students to see how the author has put together small, related thought units into one sentence. Note the author's use of punctuation to accomplish this way of writing.
7. Working with a partner, have students try to break down the text of another paragraph from the same book or article.

Application and Example

Sarah, a third grader, attended the Literacy Development Center for an after-school program. During her initial interview with her tutor, she revealed that she wanted to be able to read the books that Patty, one of her friends, reads. "She's a very good reader," Sarah told Juanita. When Sarah and Juanita visited the Center's library to select a book to take home for the week, Sarah found *Stuart Little* by E. B. White (Harper & Row, 1945). "This is what I want to read. Patty read this!" Sarah declared.

Based on Sarah's informal assessment results, Juanita suggested that this book be one of Sarah's challenge books that they could work on together during her tutoring time. Sarah said she wanted to take the book home and try it. Juanita discussed the plan with Sarah's mother and asked if she would work with Sarah on chapters 1 and 2.

When Sarah returned the following week, she told Juanita that she had read the first two chapters with her mother but needed "a lot of help because the sentences were so long." Juanita had ready a copy of the first page of chapter 3 and began to teach Sarah how to break down text (see Figure 3.3 A and B).

Juanita:	This is a copy of the first page of Chapter 3. I'm going to show you how you can better understand this author using a strategy called "breaking down the text." The first thing we need to do is number the sentences. Let's put a number in the beginning of each sentence. How many sentences do you find?
	(Sarah proceeded to number the sentences. When she got to the parentheses at the beginning of sentence 4, she stopped.)
Sarah:	Is this a sentence? Why is this mark here?
Juanita:	Have you seen it before?
Sarah:	No.
Juanita:	That is called a parenthesis and they come in pairs. One is open to the right and one is open to the left. Let's underline them. Can you find the other one?
Sarah:	Okay, there it is.
Juanita:	Now if we look inside the parenthesis, we find two more sentences. Number them.
Sarah:	There are five sentences all together.
Juanita:	Great. Now let's go back to the beginning. Let's read the first sentence together.
S and J:	*Stuart was an early riser: he was almost always the first person up in the morning.*
Juanita:	What can you tell me about Stuart?
Sarah:	He liked to get up early in the morning.
Juanita:	Anything else?
Sarah:	He is usually the first one up.
Juanita:	Can you find the colon in that sentence? Let's put a circle around it. (Sarah finds the colon and circles it.)

FIGURE 3.3A   Excerpt from *Stuart Little* By E. B. WHITE for "Breaking Down the Text."

> Stuart was an early riser: he was almost always the first person up in the morning. He liked the feeling of being the first one stirring; he enjoyed the quiet rooms with the books standing still on the shelves, the pale light coming in through the windows, and the fresh smell of day. In wintertime it would be quite dark when he climbed from his bed made out of the cigarette box, and he sometimes shivered with cold as he stood in his nightgown doing his exercises. (Stuart touched his toes ten times every morning to keep himself in good condition. He had seen his brother George do it, and George had explained that it kept his stomach muscles firm and was a fine abdominal thing to do.)

FIGURE 3.3B   Working Copy for "Breaking Down the Text."

> ①
> STUART was an early riser: he was almost always the first person up in the
> ②
> morning. He liked the feeling of being the first one stirring; he enjoyed the
>
> quiet rooms with the books standing still on the shelves, the pale light coming
> ③
> in through the windows, and the fresh smell of day. In wintertime it would be
>
> quite dark when he climbed from his bed made out of the cigarette box, and
>
> he sometimes shivered with cold as he stood in his nightgown doing his
> ④
> exercises. (Stuart touched his toes ten times every morning to keep himself
> ⑤
> in good condition. He had seen his brother George do it, and George had
>
> explained that it kept his stomach muscles firm and was a fine abdominal
>
> thing to do.)

Some authors might have put a period after the word "riser" and begun a new sentence with "he." E. B. White didn't because he wanted the reader to know that the two ideas about Stuart are very much related. When an author uses a colon he wants the reader to pay attention to what is coming next. The first part of the sentence *Stuart was an early riser* introduces the next part *he was almost always the first person up in the morning.* The second part explains more about the first.

Sarah: OK.

Juanita: Let's read the second sentence together. *He liked the feeling of being the first one stirring; he enjoyed the quiet rooms with the books standing still on the shelves, the pale light coming in through the windows, and the fresh smell of day.*
(Juanita noticed that Sarah hesitated with "stirring.")
Let's look at the word "stirring." I'm putting a box around it. Have you heard that word before?

Sarah: Yeah, like when you stir soup.

Juanita: That's right but that meaning doesn't fit here. Have you ever heard the poem:
"Twas the night before Christmas,
And all through the house

1. Try to work with just a small part of the text at a time.
2. Find the beginning and end of each sentence.
3. Read the first sentence. If it is a long sentence, look for commas, colons, and semicolons to help understand the parts of the sentence.
4. Read the next sentence. Think of how it connects to the first sentence.
5. Repeat these steps.

FIGURE 3.4   Review Card for "Breaking Down the Text."

	Not a creature was stirring Not even a mouse."
Sarah:	I know that poem.
Juanita:	Well, "stirring" in that poem has the same meaning as in this sentence about Stuart.
Sarah:	And he *is* a mouse.
Juanita:	Right. So what does it mean?
Sarah:	It means moving around. Stuart liked to be the first one moving around the house when everyone else was still sleeping.
Juanita:	Very good. Now let's look at the rest of the sentence. Do you see another punctuation mark? Circle it. (Sarah does.) That's a semicolon.

Juanita continued in this manner until they reached the end of the section. Then Juanita helped Sarah make a review card to keep nearby when she encountered text that was complex.

▇ READING PICTURES

The old adage, "a picture is worth a thousand words," comes to mind when considering ways to assist struggling readers to comprehend text. Readers' comprehension of a text is enhanced through the use of picture clues. These picture clues may be in the form of photographs, illustrations, charts, tables, or other graphics.

Young children are encouraged to use picture clues to gain meaning from narrative text. Good picture books are those in which the illustrations and text work in tandem. Many readers may find expository text more challenging than narrative because of the author's writing style and complex concepts and ideas, as well as the readers' overall inexperience with expository text structure. While today's textbooks and nonfiction books include many forms of pictorial representations to assist readers, these texts still prove challenging and require teachers to instruct children in how to "read the pictures."

The growing use of technology in our society has caused educators to broaden our definition of literacy to include viewing. As defined in the *Standards for English Language Arts* (1996) viewing is attending to communication conveyed by visual representations. The media for these communications include television, video and film, and hypermedia. For purposes of simplifying this discussion, the word *picture* is used to signify any pictorial representation.

The Power of the Strategy for Struggling Readers

1. Readers learn how pictures help clarify text information.
2. Readers learn to integrate text and pictures to obtain meaning.
3. Readers learn that authors may rely on pictures to give their text fuller meaning.
4. Readers who have been unsuccessful with traditional text may be motivated to learn because other media are involved.

Steps to Follow

1. Begin with something that is familiar to students, such as a picture from a newspaper or magazine that has a caption. Select a picture that shows people interacting or reacting rather than a snapshot of an individual.
2. Show the picture to a group of students with the caption masked. Ask the students to look at the picture carefully for a few minutes and try to mentally compose an explanation for what is happening in the picture. Instruct them to look at all areas of the picture for details and helpful information.
3. Depending on the age of the students, have them individually or collectively write as much as possible to explain what is happening in the picture.
4. Have the student then read the caption and compare it with their ideas. Since captions are intended to be short explanations for pictures or illustrations, the students will usually generate much more text. This reinforces the importance of pictures as they read and view.

5. Once the students are comfortable with photographs, follow a similar plan for "reading" illustrations, posters, and graphs. The more abstract the representation, the more direct teaching is needed.

Application and Example

Laura, one of the interns at the Paradise Professional Development School, was assigned to work with a group of five fourth graders who were reading at the third grade instructional level. The classroom teacher told Laura that these children were having a great deal of difficulty working on their social studies projects on the states because they couldn't read most of the nonfiction or reference books in the classroom.

Before meeting with the children, Laura looked through the materials in the classroom. While it was true that the text was difficult, most of the books were filled with photographs, graphs, charts, and illustrations that the children could use to complete their projects. Laura decided to show the children how to "read the pictures."

Then next day when Laura met with the five children, she showed them a picture from the newspaper with the caption removed. She told them:

> You can learn a great deal from pictures if you study them closely. Authors use pictures to help better explain what they have written or to show the information in a different way. Take a look a this picture from the newspaper. Study it carefully for a few minutes and try to figure out what is going on. Pretend you are a detective looking for clues. When you have some ideas, write them down so we can share them.

The picture Laura provided showed approximately 100 adults in a toy store pushing and shoving as they try to buy a popular Christmas toy. The store manager and clerks are trying hard to hand the toys to as many people as possible without being "mobbed."

After the children had several minutes to work independently, Laura asked them to each tell their ideas about the picture. Using a form of the Language Experience Approach (see Part II), Laura wrote down the students' ideas on a piece of chart paper (see Figure 3.5).

Laura then told the children to think about what they all said about the picture and then to read the caption she had written on another sheet of chart paper.

"Let's compare what the caption says with what we said about the picture," Laura instructed the children. "What is the same? What is different?"

The children commented that they were right about the people wanting a special toy and that the shoppers were pushing to get them. Laura then pointed out that the caption is a summary of what is happening in the picture but that the children had told much more about the picture. "There is an old saying that says one picture is worth a thousand words," Laura told them. "Look at how much you understood by looking at the picture carefully."

Tara said, "I think all these people are trying to buy something that is very cheap."

David said, "This looks like a supermarket or toy store and everyone wants to buy the same thing right away."

Alana said, "There is one lady who looks very worried, like she might not be able to get the toy."

Enrico said, "The people behind the counter look very tired, especially the man in the baseball cap."

Wesley said, "I think some people are pushing and some may get hurt."

FIGURE 3.5   Reading as Picture Ideas.

■ PREDICTION WEBS AND CHARTS

The Prediction Web is a combination of two modified instructional techniques, literature webbing (Norton, 1985) and prediction maps (Walker, 1985). Literature webbing was presented as a structure to be used with children's trade books; it is a visual representation of the literary elements of a story (Reutzel & Fawson, 1989). Prediction maps are used to chart the comprehension process of prediction and revision, as the reader confirms, revises, or expands predictions throughout the reading of a selection (Walker, 1996).

The Power of the Strategy for Struggling Readers

The strategy allows the struggling reader to predict words, phrases, or events that will occur in the selection. This is done before the reading begins and continues throughout the reading session. The reader combines the knowledge of story structure with picture and semantic clues to predict vocabulary usage and story events. The power of the strategy lies in its allowance for revision and extension of predictions as the reader progresses through the text.

Steps to Follow

1. Using a selection that is at the readers' instructional level, preview it with the students. Use the title, cover, and illustrations to prompt discussion.
2. The teacher begins the web by writing the title in a cloud shape in the middle of a plain sheet of paper.
3. The teacher can ask the students for general ideas or ask specific questions that lend themselves to predictions. Example: What do you think will happen first in the story. What do you think is happening on this page? Do you know what that item is called?
4. The teacher writes the readers' predictions in web style around the perimeter of the cloud title.
5. The students read to a designated page in the selection.
6. The teacher and the students discuss the story to that point. The teacher directs the students' attention to the predictions noted on the web. The students then confirm which predictions were correct. Together they can discuss why it seemed likely that a certain prediction might have come true, and what was different in the story that led to a different outcome.
7. Next, the students revise or expand predictions for the next segment of the story.
8. This process continues throughout the reading, as the teacher and students discuss literary elements (characters, setting, plot, and themes), along with story structure (beginning, middle, and end), and vocabulary words.

Application and Examples

The Prediction Web can be used with books at any level. First, is an example of a group of Dottie's English Language Learners preparing to read a preprimer book. The title of the book is *Secret Soup*. First, on a piece of 12 × 18 white construction paper, Dottie wrote "Secret Soup" in a cloud shape in the middle of the paper. Her students told her the Spanish word for soup, *sopa*, which was then also written in the cloud. Around the web, Dottie wrote whatever her students predicted about the book. See Figure 3.6. After the predictions were recorded, the group read the book together. As they read, they returned to the web from time to time to confirm or revise their predictions. If they confirmed that a word they had predicted was in the story, it was starred. Following the reading, the students used the prediction web to write their own story about secret soup. They could use any or all of the words that had been recorded on the Prediction Web.

A different group of Dottie's students, reading at a beginning second grade level, used a prediction strategy chart with another book about soup.

FIGURE 3.6 Prediction Web for "Secret Soup/Sopa."

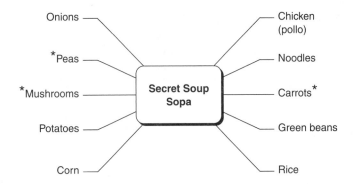

The selection was *Spectacular Stone Soup.* Using the book cover and their prior knowledge of soup, the students made predictions for the beginning, middle, and end of the story. See Figure 3.7 below. Next, the students skimmed through the book, looking at the handful of illustrations. Then they made a second set of predictions, which Dottie wrote under the previous predictions. As the group read each chapter, they revisited the Prediction Chart, confirming, revising, or expanding both sets of predictions.

	Spectacular Stone Soup		
	Beginning	**Middle**	**End**
First Predictions	It might have carrots and beans in it.	It's not really stone soup.	It makes the kids toothless when they start eating it.
	It might have rocks in it.	It won't taste good.	The kids are happy because the soup smells good.
Second Predictions	There's a map.	A boy is looking for something in the cupboard.	There's a stove that plugs into the wall with a pot of soup on it.
	There are onions in the soup.	A girl is yelling at the kids.	The teacher is cooking soup.
	The kids are drawing.	A boys yells at the girl for drinking the water.	

FIGURE 3.7 Prediction Chart for "Spectacular Stone Soup."

Teaching Aids

Each of the graphics can be used to predict vocabulary and/or literary elements of the story to be read (see Figure 3.8 and Figure 3.9). They can be used by all different levels of readers (see Appendix page 97).

FIGURE 3.8   Prediction Web Template.

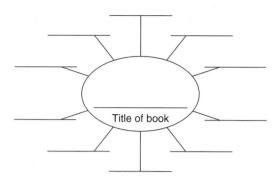

		Title			
	Beginning		**Middle**		**End**
First Prediction	Use the cover and prior knowledge to predice				
	_____		_____		_____
	_____		_____		_____
	_____		_____		_____
	_____		_____		_____
Second Prediction	Use the illustrations and chapter titles to predict				
	_____		_____		_____
	_____		_____		_____
	_____		_____		_____
	_____		_____		_____

FIGURE 3.9   Prediction Chart Template.

Children's Books References

Giff, P. R. (1989). *Spectacular stone soup.* New York: Dell.
Hessell, J. (1989). *Secret soup.* Auckland, NZ: Rigby.

▧ WHERE'S THE QUESTION?

"Do you take the bus or carry your lunch to school?"

That's a question Maria's uncle used to ask her as a child to make her laugh. When she first heard the question, she tried to answer it with a "yes" or "no," but soon found out that those responses didn't work. Later, she realized the language absurdity of the question and laughed.

As teachers, we are well aware of the importance of asking "good questions" as well as the fact that we have asked our students to answer questions that to them may have appeared to be as absurd as Maria's uncle's question. But what makes a good question? A simple but significant answer is that a good question causes children to think. Christenbury and Kelly (1983) suggested that questioning as a instructional technique can:

- Provide students with an opportunity to find out what they think by hearing what they say.
- Allow students to explore topics and argue points of view.
- Give students the opportunity to interact among themselves.
- Give teachers immediate information about student comprehension and learning (p. 2).

Over the years, researchers have shown that questioning aids students in the comprehension of text as well as their composition of their own text because questioning helps children sharpen their critical thinking skills. Teachers need to capitalize on this highly used teaching technique by taking the time to formulate questions that push children's thinking beyond the obvious. This is especially true for struggling readers.

Some teachers tend to ask struggling readers only "low level" questions because the children have difficulty with "reading the text." These questions prevent struggling readers from ever getting into the heart of a good story and give them the impression that reading is memorizing as many details as possible. While details are important, teachers can overshadow the author's message if details are given too much attention. Understanding why the old woman in the story wore a black dress and discussing the possible reasons will enhance students' overall comprehension of a story more than just recalling that the woman's dress was black.

A number of questioning strategies have been developed that were intended to improve reading comprehension. For example, Manzo (1969, 1985) developed the ReQuest Procedure in which a teacher models questions based on a short segment of text for a group of students who then ask questions of the teacher. Raphael's QARs (1982)and ReQARs (1986) help children understand the relationship between questions and answers within a given text. Answers to questions are classified as "in the book" or "in my head." The teacher models the strategy and gradually turns over more responsibility to the students to ask and answer questions.

At the Literacy Development Center, tutors are encouraged to engage children in conversation and discussion that naturally include questioning. This is not an easy thing to do because many of our children have learned the "game" of answering questions: only make eye contact when you know the answer. For some struggling readers the question/answer recitation process that some teachers use is a very anxiety-provoking situation. We try to avoid this by using a more instructional and conversational approach, which we call "Where's the Question?" This strategy was named by one of the children at the Center who kept waiting for the tutor to ask something and finally said rather exasperatedly, "so where's the question?"

The Power of the Strategy for Struggling Readers

This strategy allows children to hear an adult model book conversation over time. The children are then invited to talk about the book or story and become the teacher, as is done in the strategies mentioned above. The children's anxiety level is lowered because they see the activity as talking and game-like rather than answering questions about what they just read. In addition, children are free to choose a text of interest within the independent reading level when first learning the strategy. This strategy works best with children who have an established rapport with a teacher or tutor.

Steps to Follow

1. A child selects a book of interest that can be read independently. Based on the teacher's knowledge of a child's interests, the selection may be made from a small group of preselected books.

2. Instruct the child to read it silently in its entirety or, depending on its length, the first chapter, while the teacher follows along or reads from a separate copy. Encourage the child to ask for assistance with any unknown words.

3. Begin the conversation with some overall comment about the book but do not ask the child anything; instead, wait between comments to give the child the chance to "add to the conversation."

4. It is possible that some children will not respond the first time. That's okay. Have other books ready or go on and read the next chapter. Tell the child that he or she will be talking about the book the next time.

5. If the child is not ready to talk about the book after a reasonable period of wait time, model again for the child and invite the child by saying, "Your turn."

6. If the child still is unable to talk about the book without specific guidance, begin with questions that will elicit a personal response to the text, such as, "Tell me about the part you like the best."

7. This strategy takes time for children to learn; be patient and return to it at a later date if it is not successful immediately.

Application and Example

Tracy had been tutoring Rosa for four weeks. Rosa, a fifth grader who was having difficulty with understanding text at grade level, enjoyed folk tales. Tracy brought copies of several different folk tales to the next tutoring session. Rosa chose *The Mountain that Loved a Bird* by Alice McLerran, a picture book with text at approximately the fourth grade level. Tracy explained to Rose that this was the story of how a bird and its daughters visited a mountain year after year and helped the mountain to change. Then they read the book silently. "When we finish reading, we'll talk about the book." Tracy told Rosa.

Tracy: I really enjoyed that story. It was so interesting to see how the mountain first was just bare stone and then became so green and beautiful.
(Tracy waited for about a minute before Rosa spoke.)

Rosa: I liked the part when the mountain kept asking "Isn't there some way you could stay" and Joy, the bird, said she would come back next year.

Tracy: Yes, that was interesting. You know at first, I thought it was the same bird coming back but then I remembered the part that explained that birds don't live as long as mountains.

Rosa: Yeah, and then the mountain started to cry after the 100th time and the tears turned into waterfalls.

Tracy: It is very interesting how the author used a folk tale to explain how rock becomes soil.

Rosa: I didn't get that part.

At this point Tracy turned to the text and showed Rosa the passage and assisted her in comprehending that part of the story by "breaking down the text."

Tracy: Is there any other part of the story you wanted to talk more about?

Rosa: Well, I did like the illustrations.

Tracy followed Rosa's lead and took time to go back into the book to examine Eric Carle's illustrations and discuss how they helped relate the story. Tracy suggested that Rosa write a short summary of the story and try to illustrate it like Eric Carle. Rosa's work appears in Figure 3.10.

The Mountain That Loved Birds
by Alice McLerran

This is a great story! Long ago a bird flew to a bare mountain. The mountain was lonely and wanted the bird to stay. The bird's name was Joy. She couldn't stay but said she would send her daughters to visit the mountain.

When the birds came, they brought seeds. Slowly the bare mountain became green and beautiful.

Finally there were tall trees and the bird stayed. She could build her nest!

FIGURE 3.10   Story Summary from "Where's the Question?" Strategy.

Children's Book Reference

McLerran. A. (1985). *The mountain that loved a bird.* New York: Scholastic. Inc.

PROFESSIONAL REFERENCES FOR IMPROVING COMPREHENSION

Christenbury, L., & Kelly, P. (1983). *Questioning: A path to critical thinking.* Urbana. IL: ERIC Clearinghouse on Reading and Communication and National Council of Teachers of English.

Gambrell, L. B., Koskinen, P. S., & Kapinus, B. A. (1991). Retelling and the reading comprehension of proficient and less-proficient readers. *Journal of Educational Research, 84,* 356–362.

Gambrell, L. B., Pfeiffer, W., & Wilson, R. (1985). The effects of retelling upon reading comprehension and recall of text information. *Journal of Educational Research, 78,* 216–220.

Guthrie, J. T., & McCann, A. D. (1997). Characteristics of classrooms that promote motivations and strategies for learning. In J. T. Guthrie & A. Wigfield, (Eds.), *Reading engagement: Motivating readers through integrated instruction.* Newark, DE: International Reading Association.

Horowitz, R. (1986). Text patterns: Part I. *Journal of Reading, 29,* 448–454.

International Reading Association and the National Council of Teachers of English. *Standards for the English Language Arts.* Newark, DE: International Reading Association/Urbana, IL. National Council of Teachers of English.

Manzo, A. V. (1969). The ReQuest procedure. *The Journal of Reading, 13,* 123–126.

Manzo, A. V. (1985). Expansion models for the ReQuest, CAT, GRP and REAP reading/study procedures. *Journal of Reading, 28,* 498–502.

May, F. B. (1998). *Reading as communication: To help children write and read.* Upper Saddle River, NJ: Merrill.

Morrow, L. M. (1988). Retelling stories as a diagnostic tool. In S. M. Glazer, L. W. Searfoss, & L. M. Gentile (Eds.), *Reexamining reading diagnosis: New trends and procedures.* Newark, DE: IRA.

Norton, D. (1985). *The effective teaching of language arts.* Columbus, OH: Merrill.

Reutzel, D. R., & Fawson, P. C. (1989). Using a literature webbing strategy lesson with predictable books. *The Reading Teacher, 43,* 208–215.

Smith, F. (1983). Reading like a writer. *Language Arts, 60,* 558–567.

Tierney, R. J., Readence, J. E., & Dishner, E. K. (1995). *Reading strategies and practices: A compendium.* Needham Heights, MA: Allyn & Bacon.

Vacca, R., & Vacca, J. (1986). *Content area reading* Boston: Little, Brown & Co.

Walker, B. J. (1985). Right-brained strategies for teaching comprehension. *Academic Therapy, 21,* 133–141.

Walker, B. J. (1996). *Diagnostic teaching of reading: Techniques for instruction and assessment.* Englewood Cliffs, NJ: Merrill.

PART IV

When Struggling Readers Need to Improve Fluency

Rasinski (1989) provided a general definition of fluency: the smooth and natural oral production of written text. May (1998) defined fluency as not mere speed, but the ability to follow the writers' message while reading in natural-sounding phrases. He described fluent readers' interactions with text, as constantly make predictions about the words that are coming up next. Their eyes jump ahead to confirm their predictions, while their short-term memories hold the word being spoken. When struggling readers are experiencing problems with fluency, their oral reading is hesitant, halting, and choppy. Comprehension is affected as the writer's intent is lost in the reader's lack of flow from one thought to the next. Ignoring punctuation, the words on the page are not read in meaningful phrases. Sometimes words are read one-by-one with no logical links made between them. Other times, substituted words disrupt or change the meaning of the passage. Insertions, omissions, and mispronunciations also inhibit fluency. Nonfluent readers exhibit very little expression in their oral reading; their intonation does not reflect the meaning of the text.

The automaticity theory (LaBerge & Samuels, 1974) proposed that nonfluent readers' comprehension is affected by the amount of time and attention that they spend decoding words. Fluent readers, on the other hand, spend less time decoding because they recognize words automatically; this allows them to concentrate on meaning. Reutzel and Cooter (1999) described the fluent reader as one who reads accurately, naturally, and with relative ease. Rasinski (1989) noted that repetition, as the key to fluency, necessitates practice with a text until a criterion level is met. Although repetition may seem to be tedious and uninviting, Rasinksi (1989) noted ways to use typical classroom events to integrate repeated readings of text. The strategies described in this section can all be integrated with the day-to-day literacy routines and practices in the classroom.

Many of the strategies that promote fluency also have a positive effect on motivation. Students build confidence as they track their progress or hear themselves individually or as part of group, reading with expression and intonation. The following strategies address the issues that impact reading fluency. The strategies empower struggling readers with tools to improve their fluency and, in turn, their ability to communicate and to understand the written word.

■ REPEATED READING

Repeated Reading was first suggested as a strategy to improve fluency by Samuels (1979). This method evolved from his earlier automaticity theory (LaBerge & Samuels, 1974) which stated that fluent readers decode text automatically. The procedure includes the rereading of a meaningful passage until a satisfactory level of fluency, determined by the reading rate and number of errors, is reached. Students practice their passages (50 to 200 words) in an assisted, unassisted, or paired repeated reading model and return to the teacher when they are ready to have their next rereading timed and documented (Dowhower, 1989; Koskinen & Blum, 1986).

The Power of the Strategy for Struggling Readers

As struggling readers practice their passages in the Repeated Reading strategy they progress from word-by-word decoding to reading with more ease and expression. This builds their confidence and increases their comprehension as they are better able to concentrate on the meaning of the passage. The benefits are abundant; repeated reading of a passage provides the following for the struggling reader (Dowhower, 1989; Samuels, 1997):

1. Increased reading rate
2. The transfer of increased reading rate to new text
3. Increased comprehension
4. The transfer of increased comprehension to new text (at the same reading level)
5. Increased phraseology and expression

Steps to Follow

1. A meaningful passage (50 to 200 words) is selected.
2. The student reads the passage to the teacher, who times it, tallies the errors, and records the data on a graph.
3. The student then practices reading the passage alone, with assistance, or with a partner.

4. The student goes back to the teacher and rereads the passage; and the teacher again records the results on the graph.

5. The repeated readings and practices continue until the student can read the passage at a rate of 85-words-per-minute.

6. When the goal has been met, a new passage is selected; and the procedure is begun again.

Application and Examples

The Repeated Reading strategy can be incorporated into a variety of classroom structures. If the student is to practice alone in an unassisted model, a stop watch or timer can be used for independent monitoring of the reading rate (Dowhower, 1989). If the student is to work in the assisted model, a knowledgeable other (a classroom aide or parent volunteer) can provide the appropriate model, or a tape recording of the passage can be used in a listening center. In Paired Repeated Reading students work with partners, but practice their own selected passage of approximately 50 words (Koskinen & Blum, 1986). The students first practice silently, and then each reads the passage aloud three times to the partner. Following the readings, the students self-assess their performance and receive positive feedback about their improved reading rate from the partner.

Samuels (1979) noted that keeping a record of the repeated readings in graph form is very motivating for the students; tape recordings of the readings can also be used to demonstrate growth in fluency. Teachers can

FIGURE 4.1   Graph for Repeated Readings.

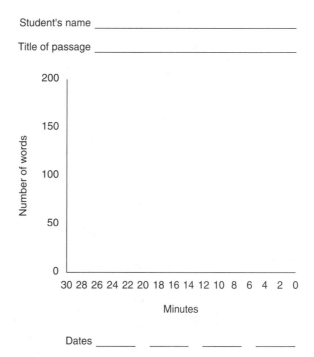

Student's name _____

Title of passage _____

involve parents in the process by sending a practice passage home occasionally along with an explanation of the benefits of repeated readings. Children enjoy watching their own progress as their reading rate increases by graphing timed repeated reading results. A sample graph is provided (see Appendix page 99).

■ READERS' THEATER

Readers' Theater is a performance of text. It focuses on the oral interpretation of the words in a script (Sloyer, 1982). Students use literature, poems, songs, or scenarios that they write themselves. The essence of the performance of the script is in the oral reading, not in the use of props, costumes, or actions. Presentations can be modified in a variety of ways. In some classrooms, students sit in a row of chairs or stools that are set up in front of their audience. Sometimes the students stand in front of the class. One interesting way of presenting the performance resembles a revolving door. All of the readers stand shoulder to shoulder in front of their audience, but with their backs turned. As students take turns reading their parts, they pivot around to face the audience, say their lines, and turn back again. As one back is being turned toward the audience, a different reader is turning to face the audience.

The Power of the Strategy for Struggling Readers

Participating in a Readers' Theater presentation helps struggling readers build fluency, comprehension, and confidence. Knowing their limitations in oral reading, nonfluent readers are hesitant to participate in reading activities in front of an audience. Being a member of a Readers' Theater group provides struggling readers the opportunity to feel confident reading in front of an audience. Walker (1996) indicated three different learner patterns that produce increased engagement with Readers' Theater. A student who communicates through drama will find this a natural way to develop fluency. Word-bound decoders, who do not identify with characters, will naturally make connections with characters through the scripts. For students who have difficulty tracking, a short Readers' Theater script provides a purposeful reason to track.

Steps to Follow

1. Decide on a script to use for the Readers' Theater presentation. It can come from literature the students are reading. It can be a song, a poem, or a familiar folk tale; or the students can write the script themselves.
2. The teacher assigns lines or lets the students work out the parts among themselves.

3. The students practice, concentrating on expression, intonation, and dramatic effect.

4. When the students are ready, they perform for their audience.

Application and Examples

Scripts for Readers' Theaters can be found in a number of places. The school librarian often has copies of scripts of familiar folk tales. From the public library, books of plays for children can be adapted for Readers' Theaters; and commercially prepared scripts are available at teacher resource centers. To personalize a Readers' Theater production, the script can be created from a text that has been read by the participating students. The following script was written by Dottie and a student whom she was tutoring. After reading Leonard Kessler's *The Worst Team Ever*, the two wrote the script, chose characters, and rehearsed their performance. Most of the dialogue was taken directly from the pages of the story, which lent itself well to this activity. The student enjoyed the practice, which helped increase fluency and build confidence. He always looked forward to the last line of the dialogue, borrowed from a movie character; and no matter how many times he practiced, he couldn't help but laugh when he got to that part. The Readers' Theater was performed by the tutor and her student as the culminating activity of the parent conference.

The Worst Team Ever
Written and Illustrated by Leonard Kessler
Adapted for Readers' Theater
by Dottie Kulesza

Melvin Moose:	Look at this.
Bobo Bullfrog:	It says that our team is the worst swamp ball team ever. We lost 35 games in a row.
Melvin Moose:	Maybe you need a new coach.
Bobo Bullfrog:	We don't have a coach. The last one quit.
Melvin Moose:	That is a job for Old Turtle.
Bobo Bullfrog:	He once won the coach of the year prize. Here comes Old Turtle now. Ask him. Ask him.
Melvin Moose:	Hi, Old Turtle. The Green Hoppers need a new coach.
Bobo Bullfrog:	Do you want the job?
Old Turtle:	The Green Hoppers? They lost 35 games in a row.
Bobo Bullfrog:	We need a good coach.
Melvin Moose:	They need you, Old Turtle. There is only one more game.
Bobo Bullfrog:	We want to win that last game.
Old Turtle:	I will coach the Green Hoppers if Melvin will help me.

Bobo Bullfrog:	Can you be our coach next year, too?
Old Turtle:	Let's see how we do in the last game.
Bobo Bullfrog:	Good job, Old Turtle, we won the game!
Old Turtle:	The players worked hard. They did a good job.
Bobo Bullfrog:	We hope you can coach us next year.
Old Turtle:	I'll be back!!

Readers' Theater scripts can be designed to include choral reading lines. Dottie's reading students always enjoy this activity. It motivates them to read, increases their fluency, and builds their confidence. After they've practiced, the students ask their classroom teacher if they can perform for their class. This is a powerful strategy for helping third and fourth grade students, who are reading at a first or second grade level, to feel successful reading in front of their peers. One of the favorites of Dottie's students is taken directly from the text of the book. She types out the text, using a repetitive verse as the choral reading lines. The following is from *Can You Carry It, Harriet?* (Buxton, 1989).

All:	(Title) Can you carry it, Harriet?
Student 1:	Here is a bee, all yellow and black, with four little wings upon its back.
All:	Can you carry it, Harriet?
Student 2:	Here is a puddle to splish and splash in, good for giving your shoes a wash in.
All:	Can you carry it, Harriet?
Student 3:	Here is a nest, snug in the straw, with warm, brown eggs, 1, 2, 3, 4.
All:	Can you carry it, Harriet?
Student 4:	Here comes Harriet's good friend Sue. Let's ask her what we can do.
Student 5:	Scoop the puddle up in a bucket. Now you can carry it, Harriet.
Student 1:	Catch the bee in a little jar. Now you can carry it, Harriet.
Student 2:	Put the nest of eggs in a basket. Now you can carry it, Harriet.
Student 3:	Take the bucket and water the plants.
Student 4:	Open the jar and free the bee.
Student 5:	Take just one egg carefully.
All:	Yes, you can carry it, Harriet.

Teaching Aids

Try browsing the Web for sites that have scripts for Readers' Theater. Here are a few to visit:

Readers Theater Online Canada (scripts for K–10 classrooms with teachers' guides) http://loiswalker.com/catalog/index.html

Readers Theater Script Service (individual scripts with tips on staging)

www.readers-theatre.com

Aaron Shepard's RT Page (lists other sites to visit)

http://www.aaronshep.com/rt/other/html

Storycart Press (a monthly subscription service for curriculum-related scripts)

www.storycart.com

International Readers' theater (publish-on demand script service)

http://www.mbnet.mb.ca/catalog/

Children's Book References:

Buxton, J. (1989). *Can you carry it, Harriet?* Auckland, NZ: Rigby.
Kessler, L. (1985). *The worst team ever.* New York: Dell.

■ CHORAL READING

Along with providing practice in fluent reading, choral reading also helps build self-confidence while students work as part of a group; and it promotes an appreciation for oral expression (Tierney, Readence, & Dishner, 1995). There are a variety of different formats with which to use choral reading (Tompkins, 1997). In echo reading, the group repeats each line after the leader. In small-group reading, each group is assigned a different part of the text to read. In cumulative reading, one group begins and others join in as they move through the text. The leader-and-chorus format lends itself to poetry and songs; a leader reads the main part, and the group reads the recurrent verse.

The Power of the Strategy for Struggling Readers

As a member of a group, struggling readers can increase confidence by taking chances without the threat of embarrassing corrections (Tierney, Readence, & Dishner, 1995). Supported by the group structure, struggling readers can make guesses with less chance of failure (Moffett & Wagner, 1992).

Steps to Follow

1. Choose a selection for the choral reading and either provide individual copies or write it on a large chart for all to see. The rhythm and flow of poetry and lyrics make them preferable texts to use for choral reading (Moffett & Wagner, 1992).

2. Read the text as a whole group several times.
3. Decide how to arrange the selection for reading. The copies or the chart can be color-coded or marked in some way so that students will know which section is theirs to read.
4. Decide together on specific intonations for individual words or lines.
5. Practice.
6. Audiotape the reading and play it back for the class to discuss what changes or improvements need to be made.
7. Share the reading with an audience.

Application and Examples

Choral reading can be used with children of all ages, from the kindergartners' familiar poems and songs to the older students' rhymes and raps of content area material. Choral reading has been found to be especially beneficial to ELL students (McCauley & McCauley, 1992). Because choral reading incorporates a low-anxiety environment with repeated practice, comprehensible input, and drama, it is an invaluable tool to use with English language learners. In addition to the steps to follow listed above, look for selections of poems with action words; and then use gestures, postures, and stressed letters or syllables to clarify the meanings of the words. For those struggling readers who are making their way through the preprimer and primer stages, many traditional folk songs and tales can be found in leveled books by a variety of publishers.

Teaching Aids

The following is a list of outstanding poets, a starting place for gathering children's poetry for your classroom and your students' choral reading. The first ten poets on the list have won the National Council of Teachers of English (NCTE) Award for Excellence in Poetry for Children. This honor is awarded to living poets for exceptional quality in a body of work (not just one book or poem) for ages 3 to 13 (Temple, Martinez, Yokota, & Naylor, 1998):

1. David McCord
2. Aileen Fisher
3. Karla Kuskin
4. Myra Cohn Livingston
5. Arnold Adoff
6. Eve Merriam
7. John Ciardi
8. Lilian Moore
9. Valerie Worth
10. Barbara Juster Esbensen
11. Lee Bennett Hopkins
12. Jack Prelutsky
13. Shel Silverstein
14. Nikki Giovanni
15. Langston Hughes
16. A. A. Milne
17. Walter de la Mare
18. Robert Louis Stevenson

In addition to the above-suggested poets, Paul Fleischman's poems for two voices are excellent sources for choral reading selections. Two of his titles are *I Am Phoenix: Poems for Two Voices* and *Joyful Noise: Poems for Two Voices.*

Also, look for leveled books, written for your primer and preprimer readers, that lend themselves to rhythmic choral reading. Some examples follow:

Title	Publisher
1. *Can You Carry It, Harriet?*	Rigby
2. *Catch the Cookie*	Scott Foresman
3. *Down by the Bay*	Scott Foresman
4. *Here We Go Round the Mulberry Bush*	Houghton Mifflin
5. *On Top of Spaghetti*	Scott Foresman

Children's Book References

Buxton, J. (1989). *Can you carry it, Harriet?* Crystal Lake, IL: Rigby.

Buxton, J. (1993). *Down by the bay.* Glenview, IL: Scott, Foresman and Company.

Fleischman, P. (1985). *I am Phoenix: Poems for two voices.* New York: Harper & Row.

Fleischman, P. (1988). *Joyful noise: Poems for two voices.* New York: Harper & Row.

Glazer, T. (1993). *On top of spaghetti.* Glenview, IL: Scott, Foresman and Company.

Glazer, T. (1995). *Here we go round the mulberry bush.* (1995). Boston: Houghton Mifflin.

Vaughn, M. (1996). *Catch the cookie.* Glenview, IL: Scott, Foresman and Company.

■ LISTENING TO TEXT

The reading of stories to children has long been an accepted and expected practice in classrooms. The oral reading of text by skilled readers provides a model of how the text should "sound" for inexperienced readers. The fluent reading, in turn, enhances the comprehension of the text for listeners. Even adults who are capable readers may need a skilled model to fully comprehend a text that uses unusual sentence structure or antiquated language. Consider, for example, the text of a Shakespearean play. Unless you are an English teacher who regularly teaches Shakespeare, chances are you will comprehend the text more fully by hearing it recited by skilled actors while you follow along with the text. This is exactly what many high school teachers and university professors do to help students understand Shakespeare. (Of course, seeing and hearing the play performed is ultimate comprehension experience!)

Listening and its relationship to reading has been a topic for research in the past (see Weiss, 1978 for a summary of early research). Lundsteen (1979) concluded after extensive research that listening is the process which allows spoken language to be converted to meaning in the mind. Many teachers, unfortunately, assume that listening is a matter of paying attention and often neglect this area of language ability. Listening comprehension has often been used as an estimate of children's reading potential because the listening comprehension of children surpasses their reading comprehension until about seventh grade (Sticht & Beck, 1976 in Gipe, 1995).

More recently, listening to books on tape has been used successfully with second-language learners in a home-school shared reading program (Blum, et al., 1998). "Repeated reading with an auditory model provides critical support—scaffolding—which enables these novices to feel like expert readers. This initial success provides confidence and strong motivation to practice, which is essential to develop skilled, fluent readers" (Blum, et al., 1998, p. 5).

The Power of the Strategy for Struggling Readers

Struggling readers who need to improve fluency can become successful by following along and listening to text read by a skilled reader. This strategy demonstrates proper phasing and intonation, which in turn assist in comprehension. When teachers incorporate listening to text on audiotapes and CDs into the classroom literacy programs, struggling readers see this activity as part of the learning process for all children and do not feel singled out. This strategy allows children to work independently for an extended period of time while building struggling readers' self-confidence.

Steps to Follow

1. As with any book selection, the quality of the work should be taken into consideration as well as the interests and abilities of the readers. A good rule of thumb for children who will listen to a book in their first language is that the book be 1 year above their reading level. In general, classroom teachers need a wide range of recorded book levels just as they do other books in their classroom library.

2. For very young readers or for second-language learners who may not have one-to-one correspondence with oral language and print, try to use audio books that indicate to readers when to turn the page.

3. If resources are limited, enlist other skilled readers from other grades, parents, or volunteers to record books from the classroom collection.

4. Struggling readers should be guided to listen to books that gradually increase in difficulty. Predictable patterned books and books that

repeat high frequency words are a good place to start. Based on individual needs, a list of listening books for the week can be given to each child.

5. Help children understand the purpose for listening to the recorded books. Most children enjoy a listening activity but may not intuitively know how following along with a reader will improve their own reading skills.

6. As with repeated reading strategy, the repeated listening to the same text will increase reading fluency. Children should be encouraged to listen to a story several times but with slightly different purposes each time: the first time may be to be able to maintain voice-to-word correspondence; the second time may be to learn new sight words; a third time may be to attend to the reader's phrasing, and so on.

Application and Example

At the Paradise Professional Development School, listening centers are established in most classrooms. All children in the second grade visit the classroom listening center twice a week. For those children who have been identified as needing additional fluency development listen to text three or four times a week. Dottie has helped the teachers develop a way for these children to keep track of their purposes for listening to books on tape as shown in Figure 4.2 (see also Appendix page 100).

FIGURE 4.2   Listening Center Activities.

Name _____

Title of book _____

Author _____

First time listening: Date completed _____

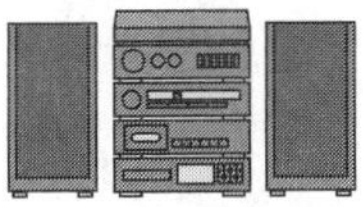

Listen to the story. Follow along with the reader. Enjoy the story.

Second time listening: Date completed _____

Listen to the story. Try to read the words with the reader.

Third time listening: Date completed _____

Listen to the story again and try to become the reader. Then read the book or a favorite part to someone.

Teaching Aids

Children's books on tape and CDs can be found easily, in places ranging from supermarkets to the Internet. Quality varies, however, and may require you to do some research before making purchases. Some audio books are not the exact text or have been abridged in some way. We suggest that you purchase audio tapes or CD sets that come with the book rather than the tape or CD independently from the books. If the main purpose of having children listen to text is to improve their fluency, make sure that the recorded versions do not have so many "sound effects" as to distract from that purpose.

There are several helpful Web sites that provide reviews and comments about children's books on tape. Great Tapes for Kids (www.greattapes.com) and Audio Books on Compact Discs, Inc. (www.abcdinc.com) are two sites that provide useful information.

PROFESSIONAL REFERENCES FOR IMPROVING FLUENCY

Blum, I., Koskinen, P., Tennant, T., Parker, E. M., Straub, M, & Curry, C. (1998). *Ongoing research: Have you heard any good books lately? Using audiotaped books to extend classroom literacy instruction into the homes of second-language learners.* NRRC, 1998. pp. 4–5.

Dowhower, S. L. (1989). Repeated reading: Research into practice. *The Reading Teacher, 42,* 502–507.

Gipe, J. (1995). *Corrective reading techniques for classroom teachers.* Scottsdale, AZ: Gorsuch Scarisbrick.

Koskinen, P. S., & Blum, I. H. (1986). Paired repeated reading: A classroom strategy for developing fluent reading. *The Reading Teacher, 40,* 70–75.

LaBerge, D., & Samuels, S. J. (1974). Toward a theory of automatic information processing in reading. *Cognitive Psychology, 6,* 294–323.

Lundsteen, S. (1979). *Listening: Its impact on reading and other language arts* (rev.ed.). Urbana, IL: National Council of Teachers of English.

May, F. B. (1998). *Reading as communication.* Upper Saddle River, NJ: Merrill/Prentice Hall.

McCauley, J. K., & McCauley, D. S. (1992). Using choral reading to promote language learning for ELL students. *The Reading Teacher, 45,* 526–533.

Moffett, J., & Wagner, B. J. (1992). *Student-centered language arts K–12.* Portsmouth, NH: Boynton/Cook Publishers.

Rasinski, T. V. (1989). Fluency for everyone: Incorporating fluency instruction in the classroom. *The Reading Teacher, 42,* 690–693.

Reutzel, D. R., & Cooter, R. B., Jr. (1999). *Balanced reading strategies and practices: Assessing and assisting readers with special needs.* Upper Saddle River, NJ: Merrill/Prentice Hall.

Samuels, S. J. (1979). The method of repeated readings. *The Reading Teacher, 32,* 403–408.

Samuels, S. J. (1997). The method of repeated readings. *The Reading Teacher, 50(5),* 376–381 (reprint).

Sloyer, S. (1982). *Readers theatre: Story dramatization in the classroom.* Urbana, IL: National Council of Teachers of English.

Temple, C., Martinez, M., Yokota, J., & Naylor, A. (1998). *Children's books in children's hands.* Boston: Allyn and Bacon.

Tierney, R. J., Readence, J. E., & Dishner, E. K. (1995). *Reading strategies and practices: A compendium.* Boston: Allyn & Bacon.

Tompkins, G. E. (1997). *Literacy for the twenty-first century: A balanced approach.* Upper Saddle River, NJ: Merrill/Prentice Hall.

Walker, B. J. (1996). *Diagnostic teaching of reading: Techniques for instruction and assessment.* Columbus, OH: Merrill.

Weiss, M. J. (1978). Listening: The Neglected Communication Skill. In Patrick J. Finn & Walter T. Petty (Eds.). *Facilitating Language Development* (pp. 108–114). Amherst, NY: SUNYAB.

PART V

Assessing Children Who May Be Struggling with Reading

Although this chapter is placed last in our book, teachers know that assessment is the cornerstone of instructional decisions. In our opinion, the most effective assessment tools are those that provide teachers with information about children in a timely manner. The more current the data, the more likely instructional decisions will match children's needs. It is for this reason that our discussion will not include standardized tests. Too often, standardized test results take months to be reported to teachers. Our focus, then, will be on those tools that are usually referred to as alternative, informal, or authentic assessments. We prefer, however, to use the term *naturalistic assessment* (Moore, 1983):

> Naturalistic assessment of reading comprehension is based on observing students' responses to reading situations during the school day. Educators through the years have given this approach such labels as "ongoing evaluation," "diagnostic teaching," "kidwatching" and "diagnosis by observation." In this approach, teachers observe students' behaviors in a variety of circumstances and with a variety of materials (p. 965).

Classroom teachers know a great deal about the children they teach just by observing them in action. For example, if a child repeatedly takes an inordinate amount of time to "find" a book for silent reading, the teacher may consider that "lack of motivation or interest" are factors interfering with task success. Or, a child who eagerly begins reading but appears frustrated after a page or two, may be motivated but is not sure how to select an appropriate book for independent reading.

Observation is not an easy task, however. Without a focus or purpose, observation is haphazard and the data collected may be misleading or useless. Mary Jane Drummond, in her wonderful book *Learning to See: Assessment through Observation* (1994), details the complexities of observations. "The complexity of classroom events may sometimes mean that careful scrutiny of one part of the scene may blot out an awareness of the other equally important elements in the picture" (p. 17). Drummond also suggests that teachers who observe children must switch their focus from their own teaching to the children's learning.

This is not an easy task. I recently was talking with a group of elementary teachers. We were discussing how to make sure that their literacy program included all aspects of the language arts. One teacher said she already devoted two hours per day to literacy instruction. My response to her: "Is each child in your class engaged in literacy learning for two hours per day?" This is an important issue for all teachers to consider and may be answered through observation and reflection.

The Literacy Observation procedure helps teachers make interpretations of children's behaviors in terms of literacy development. Observed behavior can help teachers learn about children's affective, cognitive, and conative (determination, persistence, and will) development. To use the Literacy Observation, follow these steps:

1. Select a student you will observe at least 3 times for approximately 10 minutes each time he/she is engaged in a literacy activity. Try to spread your observations over several days. Try to avoid letting the student know you are observing him/her.

2. Write field notes on notebook paper while observing. Try to record as much as possible of what you see as if you are a camera. Where is the child in relation to other students? What exactly is the child doing? etc. Do not "interpret" while observing.

3. Using the observation forms (Figure 5.1 and Appendix page 101), summarize your field notes for each observation. After summarizing, consider what the child's behavior could imply in terms of literacy affective, cognitive, and conative development.

4. Based on your interpretation, write an overall statement of the child's literacy activities, noting any patterns that you may see over the different observations. What do these behaviors imply for literacy instruction? Your statement should include references to professional readings.

In Figure 5.2 Melanie, a graduate student, observed Raymond during "reading rotations." Note how Melanie is aware that her observation is limited to what she sees at the time but that she is able to document some of Raymond's literacy strengths.

The observation of children engaged in literacy activities is one way to collect data for instructional decision-making. The Literacy Interview (Meyerson, 1997) is a useful tool through which teachers may gain insights into students' understanding of the broad social purposes of literacy (Figure 5.3). This interview is used regularly at UNLV's Literacy Development Center. Walmsley's (1991) four educational ideology categories were used as a guide to analyze the interview results. In addition, we found a fifth category that emerged from the responses of children at the Center. These categories are used to analyze questions 1 through 4.

The Literacy Interview is intended to be given one-on-one. After establishing rapport, the teacher asks the student to answer the five

Student's Name _____		Grade _____
Observer _____		Setting _____
Date	Summary of Observed Behavior	Implications

FIGURE 5.1   Observation Form.

Student's Name _Raymond_____		Grade ___1_____
Observer _Melanie_____		Setting _Mrs. Field's Classroom_____
Date	Summary of Observed Behavior	Implications
5/28/98	"Reading Rotations": Raymond is being observed doing individual reading in a group of six on the floor. He is sitting, looking around, with his book on his lap, opened to the correct story. The teacher calls on Raymond next to read aloud to her. Raymond loses his place in the book, then quickly fumbles through the stories. Teacher assists him. Raymond reads the title of the story and the first few words in a very low voice. He stops, then struggles with every other word. The teacher tells him the words he doesn't get.	Raymond seems to be struggling with fluency in reading this particular story. It appears that he has low self-confidence in literacy. The story he was reading was a repetitive story; however, Raymond doesn't seem to pick up on the patterns. This tells me that he might possibly need more experience with the story, or it is just beyond his instructional reading level because he struggles with too many words. Maybe the teacher should have made the story more familiar to Raymond by reading the story aloud together a number of times (maybe she has?), or have him read an easier story. Raymond does appear to have some literacy strengths. For example, he knows individual words have meaning, he knows where to begin the story, and he knows to read the text from left to right. He does seem to lack strategy skills for figuring out words to self-correct instead of depending on the teacher to do it for him.

FIGURE 5.2   Example of Completed Observation Form.

questions as completely as possible while the teacher records the responses verbatim. A tape recorder may be used but it is not necessary. Once the interview is completed, the teacher analyzes the responses using the response interpretation guidelines provided (Figure 5.4).

■ Cultural transmission (CT), the dominant ideology, defines the purpose of education as the passing on of knowledge from one generation to another via either an academic perspective (reading literature and sophisticated written expression), a unitarian perspective (functional literacy); or a literacy skills perspective (school skills void of concern about knowledge content).

Literacy Interview

Name _____   Date _____

Grade _____   Given by _____

(1) What is reading?

(2) Why do people read?

(3) What is writing?

(4) Why do people write?

(5) A long time ago people could not read or write. How do you think people came to invent reading and writing?

FIGURE 5.3   The Literacy Interview (Meyerson, 1997). (May be copied for classroom use.)

Response Guidelines

Questions 1–4

CT   **Cultural transmission**
"To learn my alphabet,"
"To write bills,"
"People need it for life like lawyers and doctors"
"Sound out letters and say then and put them together"

CD   **Cognitive development**
"People read to learn stuff"
"To learn how to be smart"

E   **Emancipatory—social/political change**
"So you can vote"
"To be able to know what the government says"
"So people don't think I am an alien"

SI   **Social interaction**
"Because people miss each other they write letters"
"To make people happy"

R   **Romantic/student-centered**
"Writing is showing your ideas and feelings"
"When you write your put your thoughts and feelings down"

N   **No response**

Question 5

Anthropological	(e.g., using rocks and stones, writing on walls)
Inventions	(e.g., people invented book and pencils)
Cognitive	(e.g., by thinking, to learn new things)
Etymological	(e.g., making words, words come from other languages)
Mystical	(e.g., magic)
Social necessity	(e.g., easier than drawing; to write someone far away)

FIGURE 5.4 Response Interpretations for The Literacy Interview.

- Cognitive development (CD) stresses literacy as problem solving and the intellectual development which results from interactions between readers and writers.
- Emancipatory (E) perspective views literacy as a vehicle through which social and political change can occur.
- Social interaction (SI) refers to the use of literacy to maintain or establish contact with people.
- Romantic ideology (R) emphasizes readers' construction of their own meaning of text within a student-centered learning environment, as well as individual autonomy.

Question 5 tries to tap into children's understanding of the social need for literacy from an historical perspective. Examples of the types of responses children have given are provided on the response sheet (Figure 5.4).

The children's responses, especially if they cluster into one or two response types, provide teachers with insights into their students' perspectives on the purposes for reading and writing as well as how teachers may need to modify their instructional practices to help students understand that literacy is used for multiple purposes.

Other naturalistic methods described in relationship to the four areas of literacy (motivation, word recognition, comprehension, and fluency) are presented in the following pages. Just as these areas of literacy work in concert for instruction, such is the case with assessment. Thus, powerful instructional decisions are the result of the evaluation of assessments from a variety of data sources. We have adopted the notion of triangulation from qualitative research methods. "When a conclusion is supported by data collected from a number of different instruments, its validity is thereby enhanced"(Fraenkel & Wallen, 1993, p. 400). Too often instructional decisions are based on one data source; this may lead to inappropriate placement in special needs settings or use of inappropriate materials.

During the past 10 years, many professional books have been published about alternative assessments for the classroom teachers. We have included many references that we have found helpful. A word of caution is offered: the assessment tools we present and others described in professional literature are only useful if they help teachers make instructional decisions. For example, often included in interest inventories are questions such as "What is your favorite color?" or "Who lives with you at your house?" The first question may be an "ice breaker," included to make a child feel at ease during an interview. However, a child's response of "blue" is not going to really help to better instruct the child. The second question may be considered intrusive unless the information is needed to make parental or caregiver contacts. This information is usually available in other ways such as school admission cards. A rule of thumb that we keep in mind when deciding what questions to ask children is this: What will you do with the answer? If the answer is going to make your instruction more powerful for the child, then ask the question. If it doesn't, then don't ask.

ASSESSING INTEREST, ATTITUDE, AND MOTIVATION

Assessing students' affective reading development can be done with observations, checklists, conferences, interviews, or surveys. As mentioned earlier in this chapter, observation provides details of a student's literacy behaviors. However, interpretations and implications must be made with care. If a child cannot settle down with a book during independent reading time, it cannot be concluded that there is a lack of motivation or interest. There may be several other reasons contributing to this behavior.

A list of recent reading choices made by students can provide valuable information about their reading interests. A brief conference with a student, with only a few questions about reading interests, will furnish important information for the teacher. Once teachers have gained insight into the reading interests of students, appropriate reading materials can be provided.

There are numerous published interview protocols and surveys aimed at determining children's interest, attitude, and/or motivation. Many of the surveys use Likert scale responses and ask children to respond to items such as: "I like to read at home," and "I feel proud when I read a book." The Elementary Reading Attitude Survey (McKenna & Kear, 1990) is a widely used instrument that features four different Garfield expressions, ranging from happiest to very upset, to assess younger children's attitudes about reading. This survey is particularly informative because it provides two scores—an academic and a recreation reading score—which allows classroom teachers to understand a child's perspectives and feeling about reading both in and out of school.

The MRP-Motivation to Read Profile (GambrelL Palmer, Codling, & Mazzoni, 1996) assesses a student's self-concept as a reader and the student's value of reading. It can be used to determine motivation of students of students in grades 2–6. MRP consists of two parts: a reading survey which children complete independently; and a conversational interview which is completed one-on-one with a child. The survey consists of 20 multiple choice questions that focus on children's self-perception of as readers, the strategies they use when reading, and how children perceive others view them as readers. In the conversational interview, the teacher engages a child in a "natural conversation" about fiction and non-fiction books and general reading interests such as "tell me about your favorite author" and "how do you find out about books?"

Both these instruments were published in *The Reading Teacher* (see references) and may be copied for classroom use.

■ ASSESSING WORD RECOGNITION

Part II of this book focused on word recognition strategies. For assessment purposes, teachers may want to know about children's abilities in relation to decoding (sound/symbol associations), sight words, and context. The strategies we included were Language Experience Approach, Reading the Environment, Words by Analogy, Sight Word Development through Semantic Organizers and Cloze Activities, and Vocabulary Development: Multiple Meaning Words. All these strategies encourage learners to think of reading as a meaning-making process.

Sight Word Recognition

Teachers have often used word lists to assess sight word knowledge. High-frequency word lists, Fry's Instant Words (1993), and even the Dolch Words (1953) are sources for sight words to assess those words that children can recognize within five seconds without analyzing the word. Usually, sight words are presented to individual children in lists of 10 to 20 words at a time. The teacher has a duplicate list or a recording sheet and keeps track of the words orally pronounced correctly by the child. The lists tend to be organized from "easier" to "harder" words. This difficulty level is sometimes misleading because some children may have difficulty with a word such as "when" on Fry's first 100 words and be able to read "school" on the third 100 list. Lists of graded words often accompany informal reading inventories and are used to decide passage placement.

Why assess sight word recognition? As we discussed in Part IV, fluent readers spend less time decoding because they recognize words automatically; this allows them to concentrate on meaning. The automatic identification of words and the understanding of their relationship in text is the foundation of comprehension. Through an assessment of children's recognition of the words commonly used by authors, teachers gain insight into children's possibilities of being a fluent reader.

Over the years, our experiences with sight word assessments have included the use of a variety of published lists. With young children, the Ohio Word List (1988) is very helpful. Other published lists based on high-frequency word counts are good sources for use. When preparing to give a sight word assessment, we suggest that you present 8 to 10 words at a time with directions for the child to read the list orally as quickly as possible. If the lists are graded, start at least 2 years below the child's actual grade placement. If the lists are based on the frequency of words in print, we suggest that you present no more than 100 words in groups of 10 in a session to avoid fatigue and the possible misinterpretation on the child's part that reading lists of words in isolation is real reading.

Assessing Decoding Skills

When skilled readers encounter a word they do not know by sight, they apply a variety of strategies to decode the word. Some of the strategies they use include analogies, syllabication, and using context clues. Only when all else fails do skilled readers apply their sound/symbol association knowledge and try to decode a word phonetically.

When we work with struggling readers at the Literacy Development Center, we try to determine what strategies children have for determining unknown words. One easy method is to use the results from sight word assessment. Let's say you are using Fry's Instant Words (see Figure 2.10 in Part II). On the second 100 list, a fourth grader did not say these words correctly:

found

before

different

picture

after

Present these words on individual 3 × 5 cards to the child. "These are words that you had some difficulties with when I asked you to read the lists earlier. If you take your time, can you tell me what they are? Try this first one." If the child does not know how to proceed, suggest: "What sound do you hear in the beginning of the word? What sound do you hear at the end? In the middle?" In this way, you will gain an understanding of a child's knowledge of initial and final consonants and vowels. With a word such as *different,* insight into how a child handles a multisyllabic word can be gained. Other unknown sight words can be placed into sentences to see if a child uses context clues.

Assessing Comprehension

How do you know when someone knows something? Teachers most often ask questions of their students, but teachers also know that the quality of the question determines the quality of the answer. Teachers also know that understanding can take place on many levels. For example, think about a third grader's understanding of the word *liberty* when singing "America (My Country 'Tis of Thee)" and the understanding of the word by a political prisoner. Both comprehend the word but their depth of understanding differs considerably.

One of the most powerful assessment tools we have used is "Retelling." In Part III we discussed retelling as a comprehension teaching strategy. As an assessment tool, retelling focuses on a child's ability to reconstruct the important elements of a story. Insight is gained into a child's ability to comprehend a given text, sense of story, and language complexity.

Morrow (1988) described the retelling of stories as a diagnostic tool in great detail. It has also been incorporated into informal reading inventories such Flynt and Cooter's *Reading Inventory for the Classroom* (2000) as well as a topic included in most literacy methods textbooks. A child may retell a story after it is read to the child or after the child reads it independently. We suggest the following steps:

1. Select an appropriate book for the child. A book should have a good plot structure and easily discernible events. If the story is read independently by the child, make sure the story is at the child's independent reading level. Older children may retell a chapter from a longer book. If the Analysis of Retelling (Morrow, 1988) is used, the story will need to be parsed before the child begins to retell.

2. Tell the child before reading or listening to the selection that he/she will be asked to retell it.

3. For purposes of assessment, it is best to tape record the child's retelling for later reference and analysis.

4. It is crucial to allow the child to retell the story without prompts. Some children may need some initial encouragement or an occasional "Anything else?" The book should be closed before the child begins the retelling.

5. A child may retell a story orally or in writing.

Once a child has completed the retelling, the teacher can analyze the response in a variety of ways. Two methods we have used in the Literacy Development Center are described below.

The Retelling Profile (Figure 5.5 and Appendix page 102)—After listening to a child's retelling, the teacher uses the profile to obtain a qual-

Directions: Indicate with a Checkmark the Degree to which the Reader's Retelling Includes or Provides Evidence of the Following Information.

Child's Name _____   Date _____

Story Retold _____

	None	Low	Moderate	High
1. Includes information directly stated in the text.				
2. Includes information inferred directly or indirectly in the text.				
3. Includes what is important to remember for the text.				
4. Provides relevant content and concepts.				
5. Indicates reader's attempt to connect background knowledge to text information.				
6. Indicates reader's attempt to make summary statements or generalizations based on the text that can be applied to the real world.				
7. Indicates highly individualized and creative impressions of or reactions to the text.				
8. Indicates the reader's affective involvement with the text.				
9. Demonstrates appropriate use of language (vocabulary, sentence structure, language conventions).				
10. Indicates reader's ability to organize or compose the retelling.				
11. Demonstrates the reader's sense of audience or purpose.				
12. Indicates the reader's control of the mechanics of speaking or writing.				

FIGURE 5.5.   The Retelling Profile. From Morrow, L. (1988). Retelling stories as a diagnostic tool. In Glazer, S. M., Seafoss, L. W., & Gentile, L. M., (Eds.). *Reexamining reading diagnostics: New Trends and Procedures.* Newark, DE: International Reading Association.

itative evaluation of a child's comprehension, metacognitive awareness, and language facility. Items 1 through 4 indicate the child's comprehension of text; items 5 through 8 indicate metacognitive awareness, strategies, and involvement with text; and items 9 through 12 indicate a child's facility with story language and language development (Irwin & Mitchell, cited in Morrow, 1988).

The Analysis of Retelling (Figure 5.6a and 5.6b) provides a quantitative measure of comprehension and story structure. The teacher must first

---

Parsed Story: "Jenny Learns a Lesson"

Setting
Once upon a time there was a girl who liked to play pretend.
Characters: Jenny (main character), Nicholas, Sam, Mei Su, and Shags the dog.

Theme
Every time Jenny played with her friends, she bossed them and insisted they do what she wanted them to.

Plot Episodes
First—Jenny decided to pretend to be a queen. She called her friends and they came to play. Jenny told them all what to do and was bossy. The friends became angry and left.
Second—Jenny decided to play dancer, with the same results as in the first episode.
Third—Jenny decided to play pirate, again with the same results.
Fourth—Jenny decided to play she was a duchess, again with the same results.
Fifth—Jenny's friends decided not to play with her again because she was so bossy. Many days passed and Jenny became lonely. She went to her friends and apologized to them for being bossy.

Resolution
The friends all played together, with each person doing what he or she wanted to. They all had a wonderful day and were so tired they fell asleep.

Verbatim Transcription of a Retold Story, Beth, Age 5
Once upon a time there's a girl named Jenny and she called her friends over and they played queen and went to the palace. They had to do what she said they didn't like it so they went home and said it was boring. It's not fun playing queen, and doing what she says you have to. So they didn't play with her for seven days and she had . . . she had an idea that she was being selfish, so she went to find her friends and said, I'm sorry I was so mean. And said, let's play pirate, and they played pirate and they went onto the ropes. Then they played that she was a fancy lady playing house. And they have tea. And they played what they wanted and they were happy. The End.

FIGURE 5.6A   Analysis of Retelling. From Morrow, L. (1988). Retelling stories as a diagnostic tool. In Glazer, S. M., Seafoss, L. W., & Gentile, L. M. (Eds.). *Reexamining reading diagnosis: New trends and procedures.* Newark, DE: International Reading Association.

"parse" the story (see example for "Jenny Learns a Lesson"). Then a scoring system is made for the story. A child's retelling is then compared with the predetermined story analysis, and a numerical score is assigned. Note: The complexity of the story will determine the required story elements needed for a successful retelling.

By examining both qualitative and quantitative results, a teacher has a very detailed picture of a child's comprehension and sense of story structure.

■ ASSESSING FLUENCY

As we discussed in our chapter on fluency, we want our struggling readers to decode text automatically, allowing them to concentrate more on meaning. It is important to note, however, that assessment of fluency

Child's Name <u>Beth</u>   Age <u>5</u>   Title of story <u>Jenny Learns a Lesson</u>   Date _____

General directions: Place 1 point next to each element if the child includes it in his or her presentation. Credit gist as well as obvious recall, counting *boy, girl,* or *dog,* for instance, under characters named, as well as Nicholas, Mei Su or Shags, the dog. Credit plurals, (friends, for instance) as 2 points.

Sense of Story Structure
    a. Begins story with an introduction   1
    b. Names main character   1
    c. Number of other characters named   2
    d. Actual number of other characters   4
    e. Score for other characters (c/d)   .5
    f. Includes statement about time or place   1

Theme
    Refers main character's primary goal or problem   1

Plot Episodes
    a. Number of episodes recalled   4
    b. Number of episodes in the story   5
    c. Score plot episodes (a/b)   .8

Resolution
    a. Names solution/goal attainment   1
    b. Ends story   1

Sequence
    Retells story in structured order: setting, theme, plot
    episodes, resolution. (Score 2 for proper, 1 for partial,
    or no sequence evident.

Highest score possible <u>10</u>   Child's score <u>8.3</u>

FIGURE 5.6B   Story Retelling Analysis. From Morrow, L. (1988). Retelling stories as a diagnostic tool. In Glazer, S. M., Seafoss, L. W., & Gentile, L. M., (Eds.). *Reexamining reading diagnosis: New trends and procedures.* Newark, DE: International Reading Association.

is not assessment of comprehension. Dottie has been working with a second grade English Language Learner, who is a very fluent reader at a beginning first grade level. When assessing his fluency, she finds that he makes relatively few miscues, reading with 96% accuracy. However, her student can tell her little of what he reads. When asked to do a retelling, his comprehension of a fluently read passage is found to be extremely low. Even when prompted with leading questions, he cannot provide literal meaning of the text. This is our caution: remember that fluency may lead to increased comprehension, but it does not necessarily indicate that comprehension is present.

In our chapter on fluency, we described the strategy of repeated reading and provided a graph that can be used to chart progress. The assessment graph can be kept by the teacher, but the student may also keep one as a form of self-assessment. Using the repeated reading graph provides students with a self-assessment that represents their progress as well as their goals.

The strategies of listening to text can be combined with recording of text to be used as a teacher assessment or student self-assessment. After students have listened to an audiotape of a selection and they feel confident in their own reading of the passage, they can record it at the listening center. Then they can play it back as a form of self-assessment and provide the teacher with a copy of the tape. Some teachers have the students record themselves periodically throughout the year. The tapes can be played or sent home for play by the parents and then added to the student's literacy portfolios.

Many informal reading inventories provide fluency assessments for the passages in the form of miscue analysis protocols. The one most frequently used at the Literacy Development Center and at the Paradise Professional Development School is *Reading Inventory for the Classroom* (Flynt & Cooter, 2000). As the authors of the inventory note, once a student has been unable to answer three or more of the silent reading comprehension questions, no higher level passages should be attempted. This ties into our earlier discussion of students who may read with few miscues but have little comprehension.

Another assessment that can be used to monitor fluency progress is the running record (Clay, 1993). A running record is a word-by-word written recording of a student's oral reading of a selection. For each word read correctly, a tick is made on a blank piece of paper. Several shorthand conventions are used to record errors. Clay (1993) provides a conversion chart to simplify the determination of accuracy levels upon completion of a running record. When first attempting running records, teachers sometimes find it difficult to keep up with the reader and/or to record the errors. However, with some practice, it becomes easier. Running records provide a quick, concise, visual assessment of a student's fluency.

PROFESSIONAL REFERENCES FOR ASSESSING CHILDREN WHO MAY BE STRUGGLING WITH READING

Andersen, R., Heibert, E., Scott, J., & Wilkinson, I. (1985). *Becoming a Nation of Readers.* Washington, DC: National Institute of Education.

Bondy, E. (1990). Seeing it their way: What children's definition of reading tells us about improving teacher education. *Journal of Teacher Education,41* (4), 33–45.

Clay, M. M. (1993). *An observation survey for early literacy achievement.* Portsmouth, NH: Heineman.

Drummond, M. J. (1994). *Learning to see: Assessment through observation.* York, ME: Stenhouse Publishing.

Flynt, E. S., & Cooter, Jr., R. B. (2000). *Reading inventory for the classroom.* Upper Saddle River, NJ: Merrill/Prentice Hall.

Fraenkel, J., & Wallen, N. (1993). *How to design and evaluate research in education.* New York: McGraw-Hill.

Galda, L., Cullinan, B., & Strickland, D. (1993) *Language, literacy and the child.* Fort Worth, TX: Harcourt Brace Jovanovich College Publishers.

Gambrell, L. B., Koskinen, P. S., & Kapinus, B. A. (1991). Retelling and the reading comprehension of proficient and less-proficient readers. *Journal of Educational Research, 84,* 356–362.

Gambrell, L. B., Palmer, B. M., Codling, R. M., & Mazzoni, S. A. (1996). Assessing motivation to read. *The Reading Teacher, 49,* 518–533.

Gambrell, L. B., Pfeiffer, W., & Wilson, R. (1985). The effects of retelling upon reading comprehension and recall of text information. *Journal of Educational Research, 78,* 216–220.

Johns, J., & Johns, A. (1971). How do children in the elementary school view the reading process. *The Michigan Reading Journal, 5,* 44–53.

McKenna, M. C., & Kear, D. J. (1990). Measuring attitudes toward reading: A new tool for teachers. *The Reading Teacher* 43(9) p. 626–639.

Meyerson, M. J. (1997). *Helping Students Explore the Emancipatory Nature of Literacy.* Paper presented at the National Council of Teachers of English, Detroit, MI.

Moore, D. (1983). A case for naturalistic assessment of reading comprehension. *Language Arts, 60* (8), 957–969.

Morrow, L. (1988). Retelling stories as a diagnostic tool. In Glazer, S., Seafoss, L., & Gentile, L. (Eds). *Reexamining reading diagnosis: New trends and procedures* Newark, DE: International Reading Association.

Soderman, A., Gregory, K., & O'Neill, L. (1999) *Scaffolding emergent literacy: A child-centered approach to PreK–Grade 5.* Boston: Allyn & Bacon.

Walmsley, S. (1991) Literacy in the elementary classroom. In E. Jennings & A. Purves (Eds.). *Literate systems and individual lives: Perspectives on literacy and schooling.* Albany, NY: State University of New York Press.

Weiss, M., & Hagan, R. (1988). A key to literacy: Kindergartners' awareness of the functions of print. *The Reading Teacher, 41,* 574–578.

APPENDIX

Additional Forms

■ **FORM 1   PREDICTION WEB TEMPLATE**
AS SHOWN ON PAGE 62

■ **FORM 2   GRAPH FOR REPEATED READINGS**
AS SHOWN ON PAGE 71

■ **FORM 3   LISTENING CENTER ACTIVITIES**
AS SHOWN ON PAGE 79

■ **FORM 4   OBSERVATION FORM**
AS SHOWN ON PAGE 85

■ **FORM 5   THE RETELLING PROFILE**
AS SHOWN ON PAGE 92

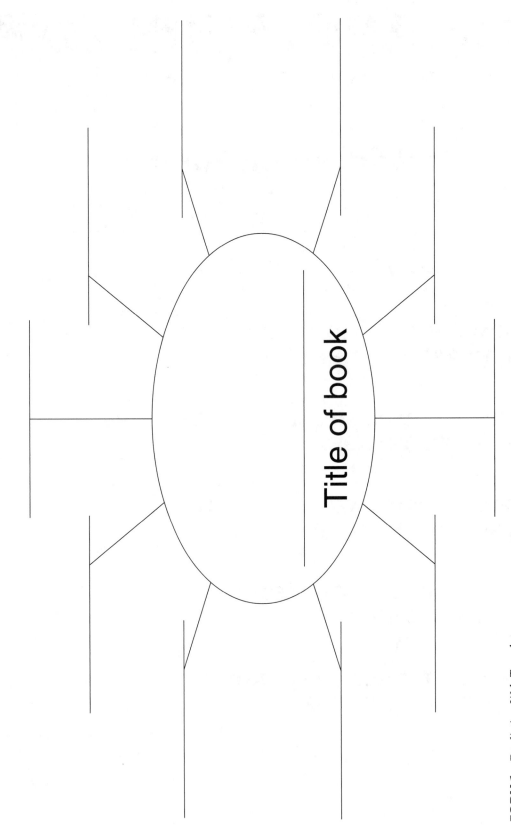

Title of book

FORM 1 Prediction Web Template.

Student's name _____

Title of passage _____

200 —

150 —

Number of words

100 —

50 —

0 —

30 28 26 24 22 20 18 16 14 12 10 8   6   4   2   0

Minutes

Dates _____   _____   _____   _____

FORM 2 Graph for Repeated Readings.

Name _____

Title of book _____

Author _____

First time listening: Date completed _____

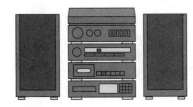 Listen to the story. Follow along with the reader. Enjoy the story.

Second time listening: Date completed _____

 Listen to the story. Try to read the words with the reader.

Third time listening: Date completed _____

 Listen to the story again and try to become the reader. Then read the book or a favorite part to someone.

FORM 3 Listening Center Activities.

Student's Name _____

Observer _____ Setting _____ Grade _____

Date	Summary of Observed Behavior	Implications

FORM 4 Observation Form.

Directions: Indicate with a Checkmark the Degree to which the Reader's Retelling Includes or Provides Evidence of the Following Information.

Child's Name _____ Date _____

Story Retold _____

	None	Low	Moderate	High
1. Includes information directly stated in the text.				
2. Includes information inferred directly or indirectly in the text.				
3. Includes what is important to remember for the text.				
4. Provides relevant content and concepts.				
5. Indicates reader's attempt to connect background knowledge to text information.				
6. Indicates reader's attempt to make summary statements or generalizations based on the text that can be applied to the real world.				
7. Indicates highly individualized and creative impressions of or reactions to the text.				
8. Indicates the reader's affective involvement with the text.				
9. Demonstrates appropriate use of language (vocabulary, sentence structure, language conventions).				
10. Indicates reader's ability to organize or compose the retelling.				
11. Demonstrates the reader's sense of audience or purpose.				
12. Indicates the reader's control of the mechanics of speaking or writing.				

FORM 5 The Retelling Profile. From Morrow, L. (1988). Retelling stories as a diagnostic tool. In Glazer, S. M., Seafoss, L. W., & Gentile, L. M., (Eds.). *Reexamining reading diagnostics: New Trends and Procedures.* Newark, DE: International Reading Association.